FEEDBACK: RESOURCE GUIDE

WORKLOAD FRIENDLY AND EVIDENCE-INFORMED ACTIONABLE TECHNIQUES

KATE JONES

Together we unlock every learner's unique potential

At Hachette Learning (formerly Hodder Education), there's one thing we're certain about. No two students learn the same way. That's why our approach to teaching begins by recognising the needs of individuals first.

Our mission is to allow every learner to fulfil their unique potential by empowering those who teach them. From our expert teaching and learning resources to our digital educational tools that make learning easier and more accessible for all, we provide solutions designed to maximise the impact of learning for every teacher, parent and student.

Aligned to our parent company, Hachette Livre, founded in 1826, we pride ourselves on being a learning solutions provider with a global footprint.

www.hachettelearning.com

Although every effort has been made to ensure that website addresses are correct at time of going to press, Hachette Learning cannot be held responsible for the content of any website mentioned in this book. It is sometimes possible to find a relocated web page by typing in the address of the home page for a website in the URL window of your browser.

Hachette UK's policy is to use papers that are natural, renewable and recyclable products and made from wood grown in well-managed forests and other controlled sources. The logging and manufacturing processes are expected to conform to the environmental regulations of the country of origin.

To order, please visit www.HachetteLearning.com or contact Customer Service at education@hachette.co.uk / +44 (0)1235 827827.

ISBN: 978 1 0360 1514 5

© Kate Jones, 2025

First published in 2025 by
Hachette Learning,
An Hachette UK Company
Carmelite House
50 Victoria Embankment
London EC4Y 0DZ
www.HachetteLearning.com

The authorised representative in the EEA is Hachette Ireland, 8 Castlecourt Centre, Dublin 15, D15 XTP3, Ireland (email: info@hbgi.ie)

Impression number   10 9 8 7 6 5 4 3 2 1
Year   2029 2028 2027 2026 2025

All rights reserved. Apart from any use permitted under UK copyright law, no part of this publication may be reproduced or transmitted in any form or by any means, electronic or mechanical, including photocopying and recording, or held within any information storage and retrieval system, without permission in writing from the publisher or under licence from the Copyright Licensing Agency Limited. Further details of such licences (for reprographic reproduction) may be obtained from the Copyright Licensing Agency Limited, www.cla.co.uk

Illustrations by DC Graphic Design Limited, Hextable, Kent.
Typeset in the UK.
Printed and bound by CPI Group (UK) Ltd, Croydon, CR0 4YY

A catalogue record for this title is available from the British Library.

Kate Jones is an experienced teacher, leader, bestselling author, blogger and award-winning international speaker. She is currently senior associate for teaching and learning at Evidence Based Education and the author of numerous books, including a bestselling series on retrieval practice.

Kate was also the editor of *The researchED Guide to Cognitive Science*, and her latest books have focused on evidence-informed and workload-friendly feedback strategies to support teacher workload and student progress. Kate writes extensively about education in various educational magazines, including *Teach Middle East Magazine* and the TES, and is also the founder of *The Love To Teach Podcast*. She has presented and worked with schools around the world. You can connect with Kate on social media @KateJones_Teach.

Dedicated to Seren Hazel Blythe.

Thank you for bringing joy to my life each day and teaching me so much.

Acknowledgements

Thank you to all the staff and students I have had the pleasure to work with at Ysgol Clywedog in Wrexham, Ysgol Alun in Mold, Elfed High School in Buckley, North Wales, Brighton College Al Ain and The British School Al Khubairat, United Arab Emirates. Other schools I would like to recognise and thank are Story Wood Primary in Birmingham, King's High in Warwick and The Cheadle Academy. I am very lucky to work alongside such knowledgeable and kind colleagues at Evidence Based Education. There are too many colleagues to name, but a special thank you to Jamie Scott, Professor Stuart Kime, Jack Deverson MBE, Professor Rob Coe, Alex Turnbull, John Jenkinson, Ourania Ventista, C.J Rauch, Matt McGinlay and Hannah Bickerdike.

John Catt Educational, now Hachette Learning, continues to support my writing. I am incredibly grateful for this ongoing partnership. Thank you to Alex Sharratt. We have worked together for years and he is always a champion of teacher writers and authors!

In terms of feedback, the person I have learned the most from is, without a doubt, Dylan Wiliam. He is regularly quoted in my books and presentations. His insights about teaching and learning (especially feedback) have helped so many schools, leaders and teachers around the world. Diolch yn fawr iawn, Dylan.

Finally, as always, a big thank you to my lovely family, especially to Geoff, my wonderful partner.

Contents

Contents		vi
Introduction		x
1.	Start with 'Why'	1
2.	Record and Respond	3
3.	Student Feedback Checklist	5
4.	Question Time	7
5.	The Detective Strategy – Dylan Wiliam and Siobhán Leahy (2015)	9
6.	Dot Marking	11
7.	Dot Targets	13
8.	Helpful Highlighting/Useful Underlining	15
9.	Marking Codes	17
10.	Literacy Codes	19
11.	Feedback Questions – John Hattie and Helen Timperley (2007)	21
12.	'Marking in the Moment'/Live Feedback	23
13.	Feedback Predictions	25
14.	Pre-emptive Feedback	27
15.	Misconception Banks	29
16.	Question Banks	31
17.	Flashback Feedback	33
18.	Non-Verbal Feedback	35
19.	Correct or Consolidate	37

20.	Retrieval Reflection Tickets	39
21.	Knowledge Organisers – Joe Kirby (2015)	41
22.	Four Quarters Marking – Dylan Wiliam (2017)	43
23.	Yellow Box Method (Selective Marking) – George Spencer Academy	45
24.	Successful Snapshots (Selective Marking)	47
25.	Pink Box Method (Student Selected Marking)	49
26.	Peer Assessment with Immediate Impact	51
27.	Precise Praise – Doug Lemov	53
28.	Precise Praise Postcard	55
29.	Editing Tabs – Rosehill Junior School, Rotherham	57
30.	Audio Feedback	59
31.	Video Feedback	61
32.	Peer Critique: Kind, Specific and Helpful – Ron Berger (2003)	63
33.	Peer Critique: Listen, Reflect and Revise – Collaboration with Ron Berger	65
34.	Whole-Class Feedback Crib Sheets – Greg Thornton (2016)	67
35.	Whole-Class Feedback: Live in the Lesson	69
36.	Student-Friendly Mark Schemes	71
37.	Exam Wrappers – Marsha Lovett (2013)	73
38.	Peer Assessment Feedback Frames – Durrington Research School	75
39.	Two Stars and a Wish (Peer Assessment)	77
40.	The ABC Model	79
41.	Think-Pair-Share (TPS) – Frank Lyman (1981)	81
42.	Read, Reflect, Check, Correct	83

43.	Gallery Critique – Ron Berger	85
44.	Flashcards	87
45.	The Leitner System – Sebastian Leitner	89
46.	Moderation Marking	91
47.	Comparative Judgement	93
48.	Hangman Spellings	95
49.	Progression Not Perfection	97
50.	Modelling	99
51.	Tell Me More! (Elaborate and Extend)	101
52.	Self-Assessment with Quizzing	103
53.	Success Criteria	105
54.	TAG Me	107
55.	SPaG Watch/Literacy Leaders	109
56.	It Takes Two	111
57.	Visualisers	113
58.	'The Feedback Sandwich'	115
59.	Feedback Journal	117
60.	Student Sampling	119
61.	Emoji Exit Ticket	121
62.	Visual Mark Schemes	123
63.	Progress Photos	125
64.	STAR Feedback	127
65.	Read Aloud and Reflect	129
66.	Feedback Acronyms	131
67.	Five Rs of Feedback as Actions – Tom Sherrington	133
68.	Feedback Finder	135

69.	Feedback Deadlines and Dates	137
70.	'Tick Trick' – Adam Boxer	139
71.	ChatGPT (AI)	141
72.	Traffic Light Collection Piles	143
73.	Feedback First, Grade Later	145
74.	Match the Marking	147
75.	Austin's Butterfly – Ron Berger	149
76.	Guess the Feedback	151
77.	Confidence Rating Scale	153
78.	'Go-To Glossary'	155
79.	Redrafting	157
80.	Spelling Logs	159
81.	Watch and Wait	161
82.	Colour Coded Feedback	163
83.	Comments Banks	165
84.	Feedback Tracker	167
85.	Chunk, Check, Correct	169

Final Thoughts ... 171
Bibliography ... 173

Introduction

It's common knowledge and widely accepted that feedback matters. It is central to teaching and learning, helping students to progress and informing the teacher about the next steps they take in the classroom. However, *how* and *when* to give feedback to learners doesn't hold the same level of consensus among the teaching profession. There has been much debate, disagreement and confusion as to how and the frequency with which feedback is delivered.

Different feedback fads come and go (and hopefully some of those feedback fads have had their day!), but despite education being vulnerable to trends and cycles, feedback is here to stay. Feedback deserves its place in the classroom, but it is essential feedback does not contribute to the teacher recruitment and retention crisis, pushing hardworking and dedicated teachers out of the classroom due to the unrealistic workload demands. For too long, feedback (or specifically written marking) has dominated precious teacher time and drained energy from educators. A shift has happened towards a more efficient, effective and evidence-informed approach to feedback, but this needs to be widespread and understood by all stakeholders across the school community.

For many years, written feedback was prioritised over other methods of providing feedback (and arguably this still rings true in some schools/countries). This was mainly because written feedback allows the teacher to evidence the provision of feedback. However, the focus shouldn't be on the evidence of feedback; the *priority should be the evidence of progress* because of feedback. Written feedback in the form of marking can easily dominate teachers' planning, preparation and assessment (PPA) time and encroach upon their evenings and weekends. It has been common practice for teachers to tick the feedback box by providing lengthy written comments on every page of a student class book. As stated, the real evidence is demonstrated in the progress students make, and this can be seen through an improvement in written and verbal responses, an increase in student confidence and their ability to understand, recall and develop. **Progress is the result and evidence of feedback.**

There has been a transition from the lengthy written comments and expectations of endless marking, but no marking does not equate to no feedback. A no-marking policy can and should still include opportunities to provide written feedback.

Verbal feedback has always taken place in lessons, from one-to-one interactions to group conversations or whole-class feedback. Younger learners can only access verbal feedback. Students with special educational needs and disabilities (SEND) may find it easier to grasp verbal feedback, with the same principle being applied to teaching English as an additional language (EAL). Practical-based subjects often need verbal feedback to guide the lesson and can often be the only logistical option.

Verbal feedback delivered live in a lesson is not without its challenges. Most notably, with larger classes, the time and opportunities for face-to-face feedback conversations with individuals can be limited. Another factor to consider with verbal feedback is the limitations of working memory. Working memory capacity does increase as children develop, but at secondary level students will reach the limits of their working memory capacity – like that of an adult. Working memory is limited by capacity and duration (how much information can be held and for how long). How is this linked to verbal feedback? The teacher might provide feedback to a student who is responsive and clearly engaged, but who, shortly afterwards, is seen to repeat the errors addressed earlier in the lesson. To prevent this, verbal feedback should be acted on, or consolidated, immediately through its recording (for example, writing it down in the page margin) and so making the feedback much less likely to be forgotten by the student.

The teacher is the expert in the room, and this is also true when it comes to providing feedback. Students are novices; they aren't trained to provide feedback, and it is not something that can be done well without any guidance or support. For peer assessment to be an effective use of time, students must value and respect the feedback from their peers, but it also needs to be helpful and actionable.

There are pros and cons (pay-offs and trade-offs) with every feedback technique, and in the early years of my career I was strongly against peer assessment. I felt this was a waste of valuable lesson time, and I believed it was more of a hindrance than a help. On reflection, I had not prepared, guided or supported my students on peer feedback. Instructions focused on swapping books and using the correct colour pen. After spending time modelling, explaining, demonstrating and sharing examples, students in my classes became skilled at providing feedback for each other. This was a significant turning point in my career, and now I am an enthusiastic advocate for peer assessment and feedback in the classroom.

Dylan Wiliam (2017) has argued that the main purpose of feedback is to improve the student and not the work, and I agree with this. If classwork, or home learning tasks, has improved then this is clearly a positive development. However, if the work improves but the student has not then the feedback hasn't had the desired impact. The secret to effective feedback is the student – the student holds the key to unlock success and progress! What the student does with the feedback is crucial, so it is important that students of all ages understand its role and purpose. Conversations and explanations about what feedback is (and what it isn't) can be very helpful. Providing time for students to read/listen to, reflect upon and engage with feedback is essential. The need to ensure that students understand the feedback and can act upon it to progress learning can be easily overlooked or underestimated, but again, to reference Wiliam (2017), 'The only thing that matters with the feedback is what the learner does with it.'

As an author I have developed a wide range of skills, and key among these is the ability to monitor my progress, self-check and correct. I can identify errors and I seek feedback from others. Through regular reflection and redrafting I have improved as a writer and grown in confidence. Similarly, when students take ownership of their learning and possess the skills and desire to improve through self-assessment, progress can be accelerated. This is also something with which the teacher can support the learner, through modelling, instructing and monitoring. There will be tasks that students complete that are not suitable for peer or self-assessment, but the teacher can use their professional judgement and expertise to decide which feedback technique to use and when.

Whole-class feedback has certainly grown in popularity in the last decade. The lack of (not an absence of) substantial research in this area is overshadowed by the volume of teacher enthusiasm. Teacher voice is powerful and must be heard. We can learn from teacher experience just as we learn from published evidence. Many teachers have shared through social media, blogs, books and events how whole-class feedback has positively impacted their teaching and their students' learning. Despite the widespread adoption of whole-class feedback as a technique, the potential for feedback 'lethal mutation' remains. As with any feedback technique, implementation and the response from students are crucial to its success and meaningful impact.

Artificial intelligence (AI) is currently dominating headlines and social media globally. There is much speculation about how AI can be used in teaching, alongside general concerns and fears about the potential abuse of AI in education. Feedback can be generated through AI and some teachers and schools are already using tools to do so, whereas others are perhaps reluctant or just not ready to. AI can support teacher workload by providing detailed real-time feedback to students, offering more frequent feedback and prompts to learners without loading unrealistic demands onto the teacher. There are ethical factors to consider however, around transparency and ensuring students know the origin of the feedback they receive. Research is currently being undertaken to assess the value and effectiveness of AI as a feedback tool, and this is a field educators closely observe and think about. AI has the potential to offer thorough, personalised, specific, unbiased and objective feedback, but the 'human in the loop' – the teacher – will need to be involved, from monitoring and quality assurance to using the information generated to inform next steps in the classroom. There is a wide range of tech tools, apps and websites that can also provide feedback to students and teachers, many of which I can recommend from my own experiences in the classroom (and during the pandemic with online teaching, they proved to be very helpful!).

When I asked ChatGPT how AI can provide feedback in the classroom, a range of methods were listed. ChatGPT concluded the answer with the following statement:

> 'It's important to note that while AI can provide valuable feedback, it should complement rather than replace human educators. Human interaction, mentorship, and personalised feedback remain crucial for a well-rounded educational experience. The combination of AI and human expertise can create a more effective and efficient learning environment.'

It is important to view AI as an assistant to the teacher (and student) while also being cognisant of the debate surrounding the role of AI in education.

After working in several schools (as a teacher, leader and in my consultancy role), I have reflected on what makes feedback effective. I believe there should be a consistent approach to feedback across a school or multi-academy trust (MAT) with aligned principles, but context trumps consistency in terms of the practice. Feedback in Early Years Foundation Stage (EYFS) is different to feedback in a Year 6 classroom. Feedback in a maths lesson naturally varies from feedback in an English lesson. The underlying approaches and principles remain the same and the practice should not be dictated by a strict policy but instead chosen by the experts – the classroom teachers.

The whole-school approaches to feedback I advocate are simple, clear and, in my opinion, easy to implement. Approaches to feedback should (in no particular order):

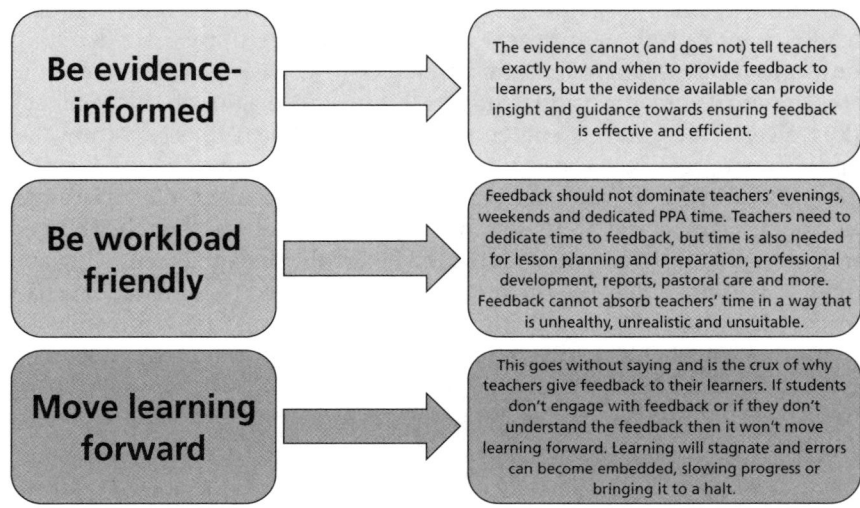

These whole-school feedback principles are inspired by the research literature and available evidence. The principles of feedback, regardless of the age of the student, subject or topic, should be:

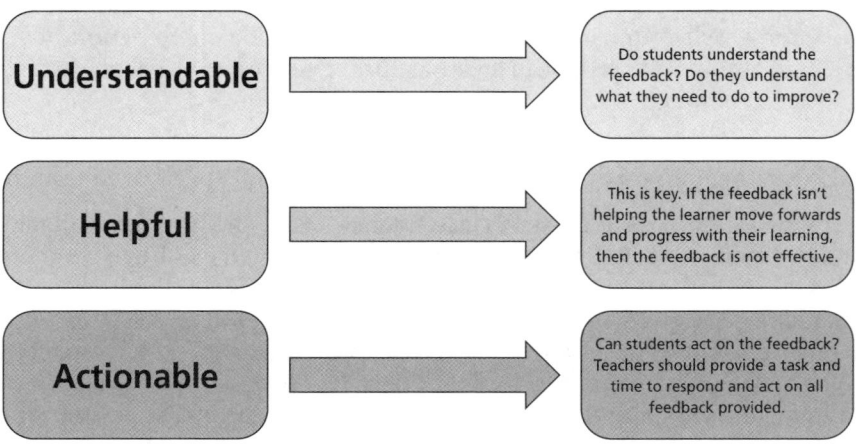

Feedback techniques and practices, as mentioned, will vary depending on context. Below are some key factors when considering feedback practices.

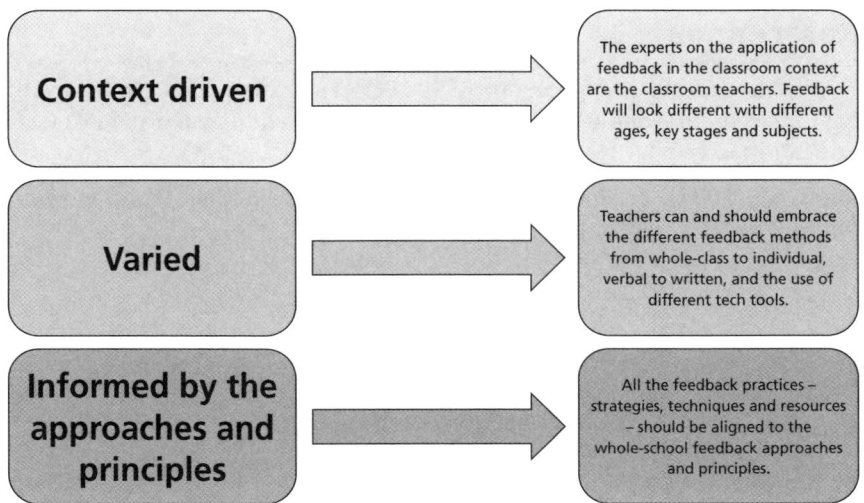

There is a wealth of evidence regarding feedback in the school environment, but this book focuses on practical classroom techniques, tips and tools. I have explored the evidence base in the book *Feedback: Strategies to Support Teacher Workload and Improve Pupil Progress* (2024). This book contains 85 feedback resources, so there will be plenty of practical examples that readers can take away to trial and implement in their classroom (and decide which techniques are not suitable). The reader will need to use their professional judgement to decide which techniques to implement in their classroom context. All the resources in this book have been written about with the suggested whole-school approaches (evidence-informed, workload friendly and focused on moving learning forward) taken into consideration. To effectively embed the resources, the key principles need to be applied – is the feedback understandable, helpful and actionable?

I hope you find this book useful. It has been designed to be clear and concise, short and snappy for the busy teacher to read and revisit. I have numbered each technique to make them easy for teachers to draw on, share and discuss with colleagues. This book is designed to be used and referred to regularly. The resources are tried, tested and trusted. The techniques originate from classroom experiences (including my own) and from teachers who have generously shared what worked for them and their students. I hope the feedback techniques will help you and your students!

References

Hendrick, C., and Macpherson, R. (2017) *What Does This Look Like in the Classroom: Bridging the Gap Between Research and Practice.* John Catt Educational.

Jones, K. (2024). *Feedback: Strategies to Support Teacher Workload and Improve Pupil Progress.* John Catt Educational.

1. Start with 'Why'

How it works

The 'Start with Why' mantra is associated with successful author and public speaker Simon Sinek, and it is often linked with leadership and business. Sinek uses 'Start with Why' to help leaders inspire those around them. I have adapted this concept for the context of feedback in the classroom. I believe it is important to explain to students why we do what we do in the classroom, and this certainly applies to feedback. Why do we give feedback? Why do students need feedback? What should they do with the feedback? These questions and this topic of conversation can help learners to understand the role and value of feedback, and so shape their attitude and response to feedback. Misconceptions and myths can occur. For example, students may believe feedback is mainly used to hold them to account or to be critical of them. It is important for students to grasp that feedback is designed to support their learning and progress, help them develop a wide range of skills and close any knowledge gaps.

Top tips

- Taking time to discuss the importance and role of feedback can help to create a classroom culture where feedback is embraced, not rejected.

- This technique can be combined with 'Think-Pair-Share'. Students can be given individual time to reflect on the purpose of feedback and how they generally respond to it. This can be followed by a pair discussion and finally a whole-class discussion focusing on feedback.
- Students often value feedback from their teacher but don't always feel the same way about peer and/or self-assessment, so again, this conversation can help learners understand the benefits of peer and self-assessment.

2. Record and Respond

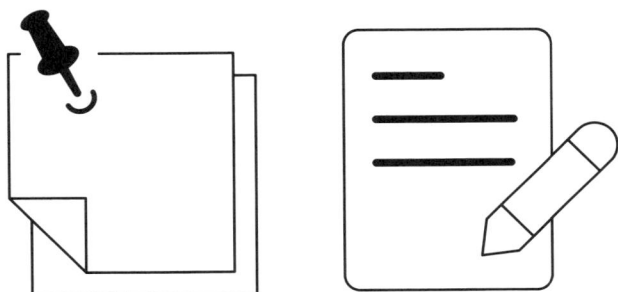

How it works

As mentioned in the introduction, verbal feedback can be quickly forgotten. A solution to this problem is to ask the student to record the feedback. The student can write the verbal feedback in the book margin or on a Post-it note. This allows the learner to have a record of the feedback that they can revisit. This technique also helps the teacher to check for understanding by asking the student to record or summarise the feedback in their own words. It is not enough to record the feedback; the student will need to respond to it and can do so by acting on that feedback (the sooner the better, where relevant). If recorded on a Post-it note, that note can be moved forward to another page as a reminder of previous feedback, and once that feedback is no longer a target, the Post-it note can be discarded. The Post-it notes are not the evidence of feedback and progress; the student and their work improving is the evidence.

Top tips

- During verbal feedback conversations, the feedback should be clear, concise and concrete. A lengthy conversation and exchange can make it difficult for the learner to know just what to take away from the feedback conversation and to act upon it.

- Students can use different colour pens to record the feedback. This can make the feedback prominent and be easily identifiable for the student and teacher.
- Younger learners who are unable to write down the verbal feedback, as they do not yet possess the required literacy skills, could illustrate it or try 'Repeat and Respond', where learners repeat the feedback to the teacher (in their own words) followed by actioning the feedback.

3. Student Feedback Checklist

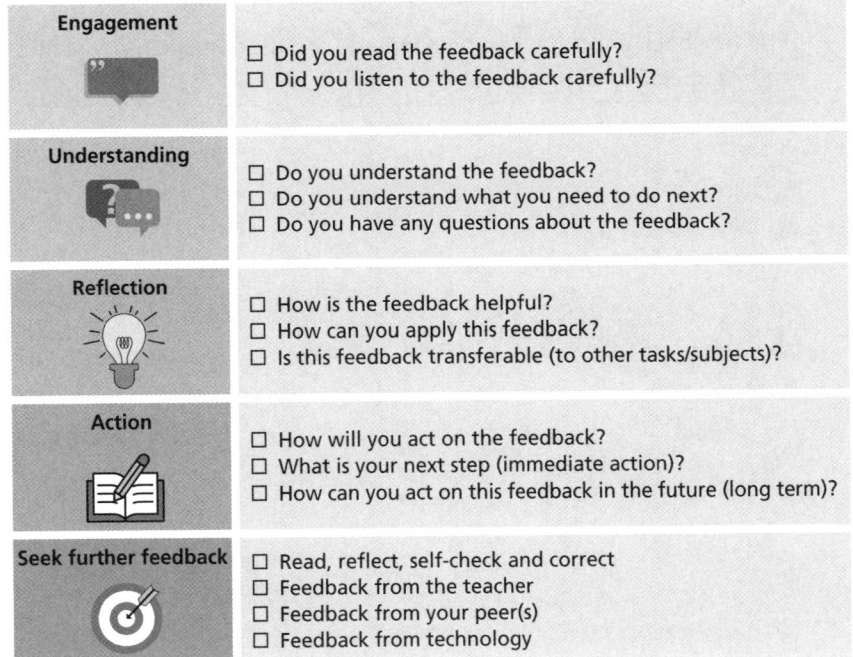

How it works

A self-explanatory checklist to help ensure learners meaningfully engage with the feedback they receive. The aim is to develop healthy study habits when it comes to feedback, so that eventually the checklist will not be required as students naturally know how to engage, reflect and respond to feedback. The checklist is a series of prompts and reminders to ensure students are actively engaging with all feedback.

Top tips

- This resource can be printed and stuck in class books, visible on display or made available on a digital learning platform allowing students to regularly refer to it.
- This can be used with the feedback the student receives from the teacher, peer(s) or via technology.
- The feedback checklist can be adapted for different ages, key stages and/or specific subjects.

4. Question Time

How it works

This is a technique that takes place during or after feedback has been provided to learners. It can be used in conjunction with the previous student checklist resource. Students will need time to read or listen to the feedback provided, and reflect upon it. If they do not understand the feedback or what they are expected to do next, then they will need to seek clarification and further explanation from the teacher. 'Question Time' is dedicated time within a lesson where students can ask the teachers questions about the feedback, success criteria or mark scheme. 'Question Time' can involve the whole class, smaller groups or one-to-one discussions. Students might not have questions about the feedback, but this is a planned task and time allocated for students to have the opportunity to ask questions and discuss the feedback they have received.

Top tips

- Students can be given feedback at the end of a lesson so they have time to reflect and prepare a question for the upcoming 'Question Time' next lesson.
- This can become embedded as a classroom routine to help create a culture where students feel comfortable and confident enough to ask the teacher questions or dig deeper to ensure they fully understand and grasp the feedback to allow progress.

- 'Question Time' can involve students asking questions verbally, but an alternative method would be the use of digital tools such as Mentimeter.com (this allows student anonymity), PollEverywhere.com or Padlet.com. Students can view questions asked by their peers and the teacher can respond to the whole class or respond with written or audio feedback online.

5. The Detective Strategy – Dylan Wiliam and Siobhán Leahy (2015)

Question	Answer
$2x + 3 = 11$	$x = 4$
$5x - 7 = 3x + 9$	$x = 6$
$2x + 5 = 3(x - 1)$	$x = 8$
$3x + 5 = 17$	$x = 3$
$4x + 7 = 15$	$x = 2$

Two answers are incorrect. Find and fix.

How it works

This technique ensures students engage with and act upon the feedback provided by the teacher. The teacher doesn't tell the student which answers are incorrect but instead provides some instruction and guidance. The learner is then tasked to review their work to find where they have gone wrong and correct errors if they can. The feedback is a task, a mystery or a problem to solve, hence the 'detective' theme. The example above includes five questions a student has answered during a maths lesson. The feedback from the teacher could be verbal, in the moment, for the student to act upon before moving on to further questions. The feedback could be provided as written comments or codes, but it is less time-consuming and can be more impactful delivered live in the lesson through one-to-one verbal feedback (it can also be used as a form of peer assessment).

Top tips

- The teacher can adapt the feedback they give depending on the student and their needs. For example, if a student is completing a written answer, the teacher could inform the student there is an error in a paragraph, or the feedback could be more specific, informing the student of a factual error and a spelling mistake they need to find and fix.

- In my experience, some students would simply prefer the teacher to tell them specifically which answers are incorrect and which are correct, so it is important that students realise this approach helps them to develop good habits of self-checking and correcting.

6. Dot Marking

Question	Answer
$2x + 3 = 11$	$x = 4$
$5x - 7 = 3x + 9$ ●	$x = 6$
$2x + 5 = 3(x - 1)$	$x = 8$
$3x + 5 = 17$ ●	$x = 3$
$4x + 7 = 15$	$x = 2$

How it works

This feedback technique is like 'The Detective Strategy' but it offers further support for learners. The teacher will place a dot in the margin or next to an error. This signals there is a mistake on the line or answer and the student must find and fix it. This is a very simple, quick and effective technique, as long as the student responds to the dot. It can easily be carried out in a lesson or after a lesson when reviewing classwork. This is a teacher-led technique, but with the focus on the learner to check their work, adjust and improve as a form of reflection and self-assessment.

Top tips

- A bingo dabber, dot stickers or any colour pen can be used. Some teachers/schools find it helpful to use the same colour pen to help students recognise the 'dot', but that isn't essential or something to be too concerned with.

- Try to be specific with the dot. For example, on the same margin as the error or next to an incorrect answer. This avoids any confusion and ensures the dot is in a helpful location for the student to refer to.

- Check students are aware of the dot and monitor whether they respond to it by improving their work.
- The 'Dot Marking' method can also be used with peer assessment.

7. Dot Targets

Dot Targets

Blue: **Revisit your paragraph, focusing on literacy.** Check the accuracy of spelling and ensure capital letters and full stops are used correctly throughout.

Green: **Revisit your paragraph, checking for factual accuracy.** Make sure you have used the correct terms in the correct context and that all facts, data and statistics are correct.

Yellow: **Revisit your paragraph and add more detail to support your points.** Consider how you can extend your points by adding further information that is relevant and accurate. What examples can you include?

How it works

This is a variation of 'Dot Marking'. The purpose of this feedback task is for the teacher to provide regular and rapid feedback to learners in order to guide their progress and identify what their targets are. The colour of the dot on the classwork will indicate what they need to do next, acting on the targets provided by the teacher. The 'Dot Targets' could be subject specific, have a literacy focus or be used across a whole school.

Top tips

- If using this technique, it is important not to have too many colours as this can confuse the learner. I would suggest a maximum of three.
- As with marking codes, it is essential that students have access to the written targets.

8. Helpful Highlighting/ Useful Underlining

> Mrs Johnstone is one of the main characters in 'Blood Brothers'. She is a working-class single mother from Liverpool. She works as a <u>carer</u> for Mrs Lyons, and Mrs Lyons has a lot more money. When Mrs Johnstone becomes pregnant with twins she is scared she won't be able to cope or afford to look after the babies because she already has other children she has to look after. She agrees to give one of the babies to Mrs <u>Lysons</u> but she quickly regrets it. Mrs Johnstone is the <u>antagonist</u> in the play.

How it works

There could be occasions where 'The Detective Strategy' or 'Dot Marking' techniques are not appropriate, such as when the student is unable to find the error and therefore is unable to correct it. This technique gives the learner additional support by finding the mistake or misconception through highlighting or underlining. The teacher (or peer) has identified what the student needs to correct so they can focus on finding the correct answer or spelling, or making an appropriate adjustment to their work. Some schools use a specific pen colour to identify student corrections, and this can be used with 'Helpful Highlighting/Useful Underlining'. Different highlighter colours could be used to identify different errors. For example, you could use pink for literacy and yellow for wrong answers, but as mentioned before, it is important to maintain clarity and avoid confusion with any feedback. The example above is a GCSE drama answer, studying the play *Blood Brothers*. Three errors have been underlined by the teacher (a combination of factual and literacy errors) for the student to correct.

Top tips

- This can be used for peer assessment to identify errors for their partner to correct.
- Some students may need a reminder to do something with the highlighted/underlined information. The teacher can stay with the student as they fix the error or return to check for correction later in the lesson.

9. Marking Codes

Maths marking codes

WO – Working out needs to be shown

U – Include your units

A – Use algebraic methods

CC – Check your calculations, your method is correct

R – Ruler needed

DDP – Draw diagrams in pencil

How it works

Marking codes have become common practice in many schools, as they enable the teacher to support students in a quick and workload-friendly way. Marking codes can be used across a whole school to support consistency and student familiarity across phases or subjects. The marking codes can also be subject specific, as shown in the maths example above. To ensure marking codes are effective, students should be expected to act upon the codes by adjusting and making improvements to their work. Teachers should use their professional judgement to decide which codes to use on classwork. A student might make a lot of errors, so the teacher can prioritise which targets the learner should focus upon. Marking codes can be assigned live in a lesson or post lesson when reviewing classwork.

Top tips

- Students should have a copy of or access to the marking codes, in their class book or digitally, enabling them to easily refer to any forgotten codes.
- Encouraging students to use marking codes during peer assessment can help them to become more familiar with the codes and can support the feedback they provide to their peers.

10. Literacy Codes

✓	Correct use of literacy and knowledge.	P	Check and correct punctuation.
Sp	Check and correct spelling.	V	Opportunity for vocabulary.
Gr	Check and correct grammar.	WM	A word or phrase is missing.
NP//	New paragraph needed.	WW	Wrong word – homophone e.g. their/they're/there.
M	Meaning is unclear or inappropriate language is used.	WT	Wrong tense.
C	Check and correct use of capital letters.	FS	Write in full sentences.

P	Write in pen
R	Use a ruler to rule off work
O	Oops! Draw a neat line through mistakes
U	Underline the title and date
D	Draw in pencil

How it works

Literacy codes are a form of marking codes that focus on literacy corrections. Literacy codes should be consistent across the whole school, although in primary, some codes might not be age appropriate or relevant for young learners but can be introduced to students at a later stage. The codes can be used to address common literacy mistakes in spelling, punctuation and grammar, which are quickly and easily identifiable to learners. Students should become familiar with literacy and marking codes, and have a copy to refer to if needed, allowing them to react to the code swiftly. The 'Proud' codes shown above are used by The Cheadle Academy to promote presentation standards across the whole school.

Top tips

- Students with dyslexia can struggle with spellings, so the teacher should prioritise the key terms for those students to focus upon, rather than identifying every spelling error. Too many visible codes on a piece of classwork has the potential to be demoralising for students.

- Marking codes can be helpful for EAL learners, but again, there needs to be recognition that spelling key terms in their non-native language can be difficult, so selective use of marking codes would be the best option here too.
- Students can and should use marking and literacy codes for peer assessment.
- Keep marking codes simple and consistent across a school. Codes should be clear and unique.

11. Feedback Questions – John Hattie and Helen Timperley (2007)

1. Where am I going?	2. How am I going?	3. What is the next step?

How it works

In their seminal paper, John Hattie and Helen Timperley (2007) advised teachers to provide the three key questions above to students, for them to consider, reflect and implement. The three questions also link to the Education Endowment Foundation (EEF) guidance report published in 2018 entitled 'Metacognition and self-regulated learning. Apply metacognitive strategies in the classroom'. In the EEF report, metacognitive regulation is defined as learners **planning**, **monitoring** and **evaluating** their progress when completing a learning task. Students can complete the table at different points of the learning process, with opportunities to self-check, reflect and act upon feedback from the teacher and/or peer.

Top tips

- Regularly remind learners of the questions: Where? How? Next steps? That can be achieved through verbal prompts or reminders on display.
- 'Think-Pair-Share' can be used to approach these questions. During the 'think' stage learners can use this time to reflect. They can then turn to their classmate for the 'pair' time to compare their answers. Finally, the teacher can encourage students to share their responses with the rest of the class.

12. 'Marking in the Moment'/Live Feedback

How it works

Providing feedback live in a lesson can be carried out in a variety of ways, as shown with 'Record and Respond', 'The Detective Strategy', 'Dot Marking/Targets' and the use of marking codes. Many schools are now adopting this approach as it can support responsive and adaptive teaching. Teachers can use the insights provided from the 'in-the-moment marking' to plan and adapt future lessons and tasks accordingly. This method is also much more workload friendly than reviewing books outside of a lesson. Live feedback in the lesson provides the teacher and student with the opportunity to ask questions, promoting a dialogue and interaction. The teacher can also check for student understanding with the feedback.

Top tips
- Students need time to think, practise, apply and consolidate before receiving feedback in the lesson. There needs to be evidence of rehearsal and/or learning prior to the feedback.

- Encourage learners to act upon the feedback as soon as possible or they may forget it or not make the suggested corrections or improvements.
- It can be challenging and time-consuming for the teacher to provide one-to-one feedback to all learners in a lesson. This type of feedback can include feedback to pairs, groups or the whole class.

13. Feedback Predictions

How it works

When a student has completed a task or classwork, before submitting their work to the teacher they should be assigned time to review their work. After reading their work, they must try to predict what feedback the teacher will give. After they have made their prediction, they should do something about it. Through predicting and pre-empting the feedback they believe the teacher will provide, the students have self-assessed and identified areas for improvement. During parents' evening appointments, if the student was attending with their parents, I would ask what their target(s) were and what they think I would say to their parents. Most of the time the students were accurate with their predictions because they were aware of their areas of strength and where/how they needed to improve (it is important to note that not all students possess this knowledge and understanding). If students receive the feedback that they fully expected to receive, then why were they not able to do something about it sooner? What are the barriers? What support do they need? Feedback predictions can support and prompt reflections and conversations about learning.

Top tips

- There will be occasions where this task is not appropriate or where students will be unable to predict what feedback they will receive, but it can be useful to gain insight of the self-awareness and metacognitive understanding of learners.
- This technique could be used for peer assessment, where students will review their partner's work and try to predict the feedback the teacher would provide.

14. Pre-emptive Feedback

Confessor	Heir	King	Fyrd
Conqueror	Battle	Coronation	Armour
Illegitimate	Soldier	Infantry	Retreat
Tactics	Descendants	Arrow	Bayeux Tapestry

How it works

The previous technique ('Feedback Predictions') encouraged students to take time to think about and predict what feedback they are likely to receive. This technique involves the teacher using their knowledge and classroom experience to prevent students from making errors that other students have made previously. This is easier for an experienced teacher, especially when the same content has been taught before, as the teacher will have an awareness of the common misconceptions, errors and the difficult spellings of key terms. By using this insight, and sharing it with students, they can try to prevent their classes from repeating those mistakes. The example above is from my Year 7 classroom focusing on spellings (but 'Pre-emptive Feedback' could look different depending on the classroom context). I noticed Year 7 students struggled to spell the key words shown (they are challenging subject-specific terms). I created a spelling word list resource (a 'Knowledge Organiser' could be used) for my class and regularly encouraged students to refer to the list and check (correct if necessary) the spellings of the tier three vocabulary. This led to students spelling the key terms correctly, allowing my feedback to be focused elsewhere.

Top tips

- 'Pre-emptive Feedback' embraces the concept of 'prevention is better than cure'. Using teacher insight and expertise can help prevent students from making mistakes before they happen.
- Early career teachers/newly qualified teachers/probation teachers and non-specialists can ask experienced colleagues for advice about the common errors and misconceptions that arise within specific topics and units, so they can prepare to support their learners with 'Pre-emptive Feedback'.

15. Misconception Banks

 **English Literature: Misconceptions Bank
Frankenstein**

- Frankenstein is the name of the scientist, not the monster, but students can get confused by this as the monster has no name.

- Victor Frankenstein did not live in a grand castle. This misconception has been created through film versions of the story.

- Frankenstein was not a 'crazy, old scientist'; he was young, intelligent and ambitious.

- 'The monster is stupid.' This is not true in the text but is how the monster is viewed in stage and film productions, and this misconception has become embedded in modern culture.

- Frankenstein created an 'evil monster'. The monster was initially innocent until learning about death and destruction from mankind.

How it works

Learners' misconceptions can vary, but when content, topics or themes are revisited (with different classes or over multiple academic years) some misconceptions appear again and again. Through keeping a record of common student misconceptions, as shown in the example above with a 'Misconceptions Bank' resource, it can increase teacher awareness of misconceptions. Instead of the teacher giving feedback on the same mistakes repeated by different students, the teacher can tackle and address the misconception early on. This valuable resource can be used as a form of 'Pre-emptive Feedback', as the teacher is preventing the students from making a mistake in the first place rather than simply providing feedback after the mistake has occurred.

Top tips

- The teacher can refer to 'Misconception Banks' when planning, designing and delivering lessons.
- This resource can be particularly valuable when teaching curriculum content for the first time as an early career teacher or non-specialist.

16. Question Banks

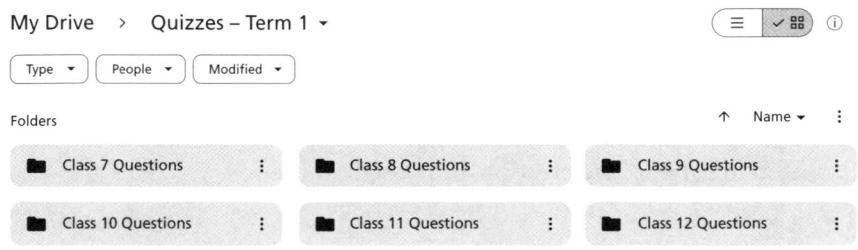

How it works

A 'Question Bank' contains a collection of essential questions that all learners should be able to answer. The correct answers should be included alongside the questions within the bank, and it is these answers that can be used as a feedback resource. All staff should have access to the 'Question Banks'. They can be created collaboratively, or topics can be divided and delegated to members of staff. The questions will focus on the core curriculum content and knowledge, and include information students are required to know, from key facts to significant dates, regarding individuals, quotes or vocabulary. 'Question Banks' can be presented as quiz sheets with questions and answers provided to support in-class, paired or self-quizzing. 'Question Banks' could also be shared with parents to encourage quizzing outside the classroom, which enables the parent to ask relevant questions and use the answer sheet to provide immediate feedback.

Top tips

- If working in a small school or department, it can be helpful to collaborate with other schools in the local area or across a MAT.
- If regularly referred to and used in a variety of ways, they can become an integral element of curriculum design, lesson planning and formative assessment.
- The 'Question Banks' can be digital or paper resources. AI can be used to support the creation and design of them.

17. Flashback Feedback

 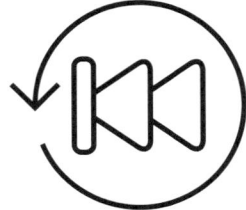

How it works

Reminding students to revisit feedback is something teachers do regularly, but revisiting feedback is not something that students do instinctively (although I have known some learners to demonstrate this). This activity is very simple and quick. It encourages students to go back through their book, class notes or folder and find feedback that was given to them previously (this could be feedback from the teacher, peer or from a digital source). The students then need to consider if they have responded to that feedback or if they have reverted to making the same errors and mistakes. The flashback is a reminder of feedback so that it is at the forefront of their minds so that students are aware of what they need to do and how they can improve. This should prevent the teacher from providing the learner with the same feedback repeatedly, because the flashback has provided the reminder and nudged the learner in the right direction!

> **Top tips**
> - By regularly embedding this as a classroom routine, students can develop the study habit of revisiting and reviewing feedback. This helps to ensure the feedback has improved the student and not just the work.

Feedback: Resource Guide

- This can be linked to other feedback techniques, such as 'Record and Respond' (technique 2), where students collect a previous Post-it note containing teacher feedback that they recorded, and keep it visible in the lesson as a visual reminder of their target.
- Students can keep a record of feedback in their class book or in a feedback log/journal (technique 59) as a learning aid that they regularly consult to monitor their progress and inform next steps.

18. Non-Verbal Feedback

How it works

Non-verbal feedback can include facial expressions, hand and body gestures, eye contact and subtle body language as a method of communicating with learners. This is an underrated and undervalued teacher skill that is not as widely discussed as other methods of feedback. Non-verbal feedback is associated with younger learners, especially when they do not yet possess the skills and abilities to understand verbal and/or written feedback. However, it is not just younger learners that can respond well to non-verbal feedback, and it can be used in any classroom. Hand signals and movements can encourage elaboration or promote a change in direction or response.

Top tips

- If you can observe an Early Years Foundation Stage (EYFS) lesson (I encourage you to do so!), it is likely you will notice how the EYFS practitioners are highly skilled at providing non-verbal feedback, prompts, encouragement and instructions to their classes.
- It is important that students are aware of non-verbal communication and gestures, and that they pay attention to the teacher when required.

- Gestures such as nodding and smiling can be very encouraging for learners, but it is important not to give mixed messages or confusing cues (for example, smiling and nodding when a student is incorrect). However, an incorrect answer obviously does not have to be met with a frown; instead, use other non-verbal or verbal prompts and cues.

19. Correct or Consolidate

Spelling		Correct or consolidate
Rain	✔	Rain
Wayte	✗	Wait
Paid	✔	Paid

How it works

I observed this feedback technique in a Year 1 lesson at Story Wood School in Birmingham (where I am a governor at the school). The class had completed a spelling test, and the teacher was spelling out the key words for the students to check. If the student had spelled the key word correctly, they would mark a tick (using their purple pen) next to the word, or a cross if the spelling was incorrect. This is a good form of self-assessment as students can see what they have spelled correctly or incorrectly. However, if the students simply put an X next to an incorrect spelling, they could continue to spell the word incorrectly. It is important they record the accurate spelling to identify the mistake they made. In this lesson I was observing, the teacher instructed everyone in the class to write the word again, on the same line, using their purple pen. If they spelled the word correctly, then they were writing it out again to consolidate. If they spelled the word incorrectly, they were practising the correct spelling. This also avoids singling out students by only asking the students who answered incorrectly to write out the word again. Everyone in the class writes the word again, and it is useful practice for all. This had clearly become a well-established routine as students knew they were required to write the word again to 'Correct or Consolidate'.

Top tips

- Using a specific colour pen can be helpful (although not essential) for making corrections stand out – visible for the student and teacher.
- This feedback task can be used with quizzing, such as a 'Do Now' task in addition to support spellings.

20. Retrieval Reflection Tickets

Areas of strength (accuracy and confidence)	Areas for improvement (gaps in my knowledge)
• I remembered lots of correct information about the Buddha, Siddhartha Gautama, known as 'the enlightened one'. • I can confidently explain the Four Noble Truths and the beliefs about suffering in Buddhism. • I can explain in detail the concept of reincarnation and what followers of Buddhism believe about this. • I know the key words mantra, enlightenment, anatta and anicca and what they mean.	• I forgot what the Five Precepts are. I need to check my knowledge organiser because I have forgotten this twice. I know some of them but not all of them. • I wasn't able to answer the questions about the Buddhist temple. I was absent when this was taught in the lesson so I need to read the class notes Miss gave me. • I forgot what the Middle Way meant but I now know this and when we do the quiz next time, I think I will get this right!

How it works

I originally created this resource as a 'Retrieval Reflection Ticket'; however, it can be used at the end of a lesson after checking for understanding or after a summative assessment. The main purpose of the 'Retrieval Reflection Ticket' is for students to engage with the feedback, instead of focusing on a score, grade or percentage. For example, after a 'Do Now' quiz at the start of a lesson, students can make a quick note of the questions they feel confident about and answered correctly but also record any gaps in knowledge. If students complete quizzes but do not meaningfully engage with the feedback, then they risk repeating the same errors and not identifying and closing the knowledge gaps. The 'Retrieval Reflection Ticket' can be used to support the student and the teacher with areas of focus and next steps.

Top tips

- The ticket can be completed on paper, in class books or on a digital document.
- Skim-read all the 'Retrieval Reflection Tickets' and make a note of common mistakes and shared gaps in knowledge. Use this information to support future lesson planning and responsive teaching.
- A third column could be added focusing on what the student will do next.
- Students could be instructed to discuss the recorded points with a partner, telling one another their areas of strength and areas for development. This allows for the verbalisation of students' reflections.

21. Knowledge Organisers – Joe Kirby (2015)

How it works

A 'Knowledge Organiser' (KO), devised by teacher and school leader Joe Kirby, is a single document that contains key curriculum content for a unit or topic (if you are not familiar with a KO, there are lots of examples available to view online). A KO can be very helpful for communicating and sharing important information with learners, but it should also be used by students to consolidate knowledge and provide opportunities for retrieval practice. A KO can and should be used to provide feedback. Students can use a KO to self-check and correct their work. A KO can be used to provide feedback to learners from their peers with paired quizzing. A KO can also enable and encourage parents to ask their child(ren) questions and use the information included to provide immediate feedback.

Top tips

- If students are not instructed on how to use and review their KO, it can potentially become a disregarded document offering little (or no) value and support to move learning forwards.

- If including vocabulary on a KO, be sure to include definitions as learners may confuse key terms. The definitions can also be used to provide feedback to learners through peer or self-assessment.
- AI can be used to create a KO, in addition to creating quiz questions based on the content of the KO. The KO itself is the answer sheet for students to refer to. Bear in mind that AI can be used to generate a KO, but the teacher should aim to include a detailed prompt and quality assure to check for any errors.

22. Four Quarters Marking – Dylan Wiliam (2017)

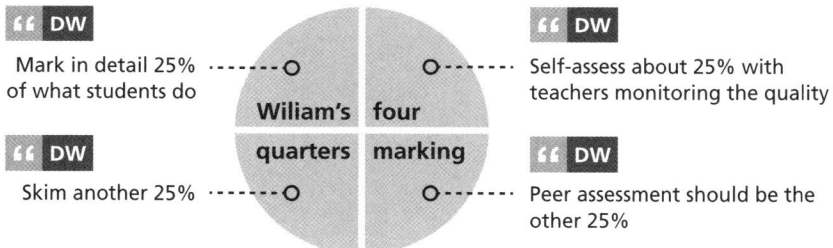

How it works

The 'Four Quarters Marking' model by Dylan Wiliam (2017) provides guidance about feedback and can offer a solution to the workload burden caused by excessive marking. According to Wiliam, classroom teachers should mark 25% of classwork in detail. Another 25% of students' work can be skimmed to check for understanding, ensure accountability of the learners and identify areas for development. Students should self-assess about 25% of classwork (with the teacher supporting and monitoring the quality of that assessment). The final quarter should be represented by peer assessment (again with accompanying explicit instruction and support from the teacher). This helps to promote consistency across a department and enables transparency as all stakeholders know what type of feedback will be provided and when.

Feedback: Resource Guide

> **Top tips**
>
> - It is important to consider the nuances across key stages and subjects, as younger learners will not be able to access and understand detailed marking. Subjects like maths are likely to draw on more self-assessment opportunities.
> - The marking proportions (expressed as percentages) should be regarded as a guide, not a non-negotiable. Context takes priority over consistency with feedback approaches and techniques.

23. Yellow Box Method (Selective Marking) – George Spencer Academy

When? Include a specific date.

> Eating in the past.   *Sp. supermar_ets*
> Back then, there were no supermarets, so people either grew or hunted their own food. On the farm they grew vegetables, such as cabbages and potatoes, and they also used milk from their cows to make butter and cream. In the towns, there were shops where you could buy bacon, eggs, cheese and bread. Cooking equipment was quite different than it is today. Lots of people had open

Good examples. Can you add one more?

How it works

This selective marking approach is known as the 'Yellow Box Method'; a simple and workload-friendly option for providing individual written feedback. This approach should be used with classwork or practice exam answers rather than summative assessments. When reviewing students' written work, the teacher will read all of the work submitted but only select a paragraph or section on which to provide feedback, in contrast to marking all of the content. This section is then outlined with the yellow box, and content outside of the box is not commented upon. This enables the teacher to provide focused feedback but to do so in a quicker way than with traditional marking methods. Only the section identified by the teacher with a yellow box must be rewritten by the student, acting upon the feedback provided to adjust and improve. The teacher can combine written comments with marking codes within the yellow box. This is particularly useful in subjects where students are required to write lengthy essays, such as in English and humanities.

> **Top tips**
>
> - The box does not have to be yellow, but colour consistency can support students to recognise the approach, and the colour should be bold to be easily identifiable.
> - This method can also be used for peer assessment.

24. Successful Snapshots (Selective Marking)

> Tourism is travel away from home for leisure, usually involving an overnight stay. Domestic tourism is when people travel within their own country, while international tourism is when people travel abroad.
> Benefits. Tourism can bring many benefits to an area. Tourists spend money in local shops, hotels and restaurants, which creates jobs and

How it works

This idea was inspired by and is directly linked to the 'Yellow Box Method'; however, the focus is different. Where the 'Yellow Box Method' highlights the actionable task, the purpose of the 'Successful Snapshot' is to highlight a key strength or section, thereby demonstrating excellence. When using a selective marking approach, teachers tend to select the weakest paragraph (or section) for students to improve. It is possible to identify strengths in the yellow box selection, but the focus tends to be on the corrections required. For the teacher to single out the weakest part of classwork, and not recognise or address the strongest part, can understandably be frustrating for the learner. The 'Successful Snapshots' approach highlights areas of strength, which helps to improve student confidence. I recommend using a different colour pen, simply to make the distinction from the 'Yellow Box Method', the contents of which the learners are expected to redo or improve. The snapshot box doesn't require further improvements; it is simply there to add recognition and precise praise.

Top tips

- Students can be asked to reflect on and answer the following question: 'Why do you think that section of work was picked as the successful snapshot?' This allows learners to reflect on their work and identify the areas of strength.
- This can also be used with peer assessment.

25. Pink Box Method (Student Selected Marking)

1) $3x + 5 = 14$
   $x = 3$

2) $2y - 7 = 11$
   $y = 9$

3) $2y = 3$
   $y = 9$

4) $5a4 = 4$
   $a = 8$

How it works

This is another technique resembling the 'Yellow Box Method'; however, the main difference here is not the colour used but the ownership students are given over their work as they select a specific section on which they would like feedback (or further support). This can take place during a lesson or after work has been completed. The student will use a pink highlighter (or any colour to make the box identifiable) to draw a box around a section of work they would like the teacher to review and provide feedback on. This could be a paragraph of an extended piece of writing where students are lacking confidence and would benefit from guidance and feedback. The pink box could be drawn around questions that the students have answered but with which they might need support or clarification. This can be very powerful as it provides the learners with an opportunity to reflect, select and share with their teacher where they feel they would benefit from teacher feedback (this could be used with peer assessment too).

Top tips

- This task works well after self-assessment. Students can self-assess answers, but if they require further help, they can use the 'Pink Box Method' to communicate this to their teacher.
- This can be optional or students can be instructed to select a section of their work upon which they would like to receive feedback.
- This can lead to insightful conversations and questions. For example, 'Tell me why you selected this part of your work with a pink box.'

26. Peer Assessment with Immediate Impact

> Sp
> It was a cold and dark night, the wind was whistling and the trees were swaying from side to side. It was the middle of January and the sea side village was deserted because the tourists don't arrive until spring and the locals were tucked up warm in *bed* It was always the same in the winter but tonight was different, the people had no idea that their life was about to change forever.
> FS   FS
>
> WWW – Excellent description to set the scene and atmosphere, a great cliffhanger in the opening to keep the reader curious – I want to read more!
>
> EBI – Use a variety of sentence starters in your story, not just 'It was ...' Your next paragraph should be longer. That was a short paragraph to set the scene, but you now need to introduce the main character or characters.

How it works

Most peer assessment that takes place with extended pieces of writing tends to occur after the written task is completed, but this approach can minimise the impact of that feedback. In a lesson where an extended written task is taking place, the teacher is often unable to continually provide feedback to students (for example, after each paragraph) as there are too many students and not enough time. However, this approach can be used as a form of peer assessment, with students regularly providing feedback to one another – throughout the process, not at its end. This approach can be used to maximise feedback with immediate impact. After each paragraph (or response), students swap work and provide feedback. Their partner can then act upon this feedback as they continue to complete the task, as shown in the example above. An important aspect of formative assessment is that it is continually happening during the learning process and not just after a task is completed when it is too late for the student to engage with and respond to the peer feedback.

> **Top tips**
>
> - For this or any example of peer assessment to be effective, it is important that students are trained on how to provide and receive feedback to and from their peers.
> - The teacher can regularly monitor the peer assessment and offer guidance and support.
> - The feedback that students provide to each other can be written or verbal, or both.

27. Precise Praise – Doug Lemov

> Excellent pronunciation of the school subjects and accurate use of the past tense!

How it works

Generic praise and comments such as 'Great job!' show appreciation, but they do not provide any feedback to move learning forward. There can be a place in the classroom for those comments as a form of recognition, but meaningful feedback must be provided too. Author of *Teach Like a Champion 3.0*, Doug Lemov (2021), writes about 'Precise Praise' in the classroom. Lemov advises that when praise is given to students it should be clearly explained what the praise is targeting, as shown in the MFL (modern foreign languages) example above. If the praise is precise, students have something concrete to continue to be proud of. This can also make the required areas for improvement clearer to identify and understand. 'Precise Praise' is relevant to verbal and written feedback.

Top tips

- Using generic praise can be a hard habit to kick and one a teacher can slip back into without realising (I speak from experience!). A colleague or observer can help to identify and focus on 'Precise Praise' through informal lesson visits and learning walks.

- 'Precise Praise' can and should be used with peer assessment and feedback. This can be combined with other techniques such as 'Two Stars and a Wish' (technique 39) and the 'Feedback Sandwich' (technique 58).
- 'Comments Banks' (see technique 83) can be useful to create with a range of relevant 'Precise Praise' examples and statements to select and award.

28. Precise Praise Postcard

Subject:

Name:

Precise Praise:

Signed:

How it works

This resource was inspired by the work of Doug Lemov and designed to celebrate student success. The postcard provides feedback to the student and their parents. Praise postcards often contain a generic congratulatory message, whereas a 'Precise Praise Postcard' is designed to provide specific feedback focusing on the student's success and achievement(s). I was once visiting a primary school and was given five blank praise postcards. Throughout the day I was encouraged to give these to students who had impressed me or demonstrated any of the school's values. As an external visitor this was lovely for me to do, and the students receiving the postcard were very pleased! The 'Precise Praise Postcard' can be linked to academic progress or can be awarded in recognition of a specific act of kindness or demonstrating school values.

> **Top tips**
>
> - A generic template can be created across a whole school, phase or department. They can be linked to house points and any rewards systems already in place.
> - This method can be used with peer assessment where students fill in a 'Precise Praise Postcard' template that they can give to their peers.
> - The postcard can be paper format or a digital version that is sent to parents electronically.

29. Editing Tabs – Rosehill Junior School, Rotherham

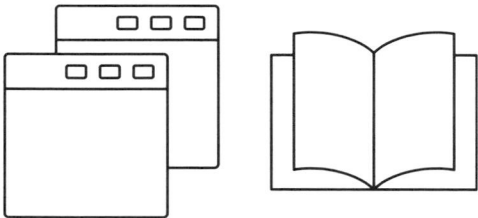

How it works

'Editing Tabs', also referred to as 'editing flaps', is a redrafting technique where students redraft a section of their classwork (this can be part of a story, an exam answer or something else), and the redrafted version is completed on a different section of paper that is then attached above the original piece of work. This 'Editing Tab' should not be used to completely cover the original piece of classwork, but instead be glued into the margin. The redrafted work can be lifted to reveal the original work underneath thus allowing comparison. This enables the student, teacher and parent to observe the progress through acting on feedback and redrafting work. It is a visible way of demonstrating redrafting, acting on feedback and making progress.

> ### Top tips
> - This technique can be combined with the 'Yellow Box Method' (see technique 23).
> - This can be adapted for a digital version where previous versions are available to view.

Feedback: Resource Guide

- 'Editing Tabs' could be used alongside peer assessment, where a student has revised and redrafted their work based on the feedback from their peer(s).
- There are examples of 'Editing Tabs' online. Amjad Ali has a blog post dedicated to this feedback technique at www.trythisteaching.com/2016/12/editing-tabs/.

30. Audio Feedback

How it works

I began using 'Audio Feedback' during the pandemic with online learning. It provided a solution to a problem but also revealed many benefits. 'Audio Feedback' offers the advantages of verbal feedback as it is quicker than written feedback, and it allows the student to listen to the teacher's tone of voice. However, unlike verbal feedback that can be forgotten, students can replay the recording to revisit or remind themselves of the feedback. 'Audio Feedback' also enables the teacher to provide verbal feedback outside of a lesson or when a student is not present. Parents, colleagues and line managers can also listen to the feedback as they wish. This feedback can be provided to individual learners, pairs or groups or used for whole-class feedback. Students with SEND or EAL learners can also find this technique helpful.

Top tips

- There are tools and apps that can support teachers with 'Audio Feedback', and a great example of these is Vibbl. To find out more information visit Vibbl.com.

- As with any type of feedback, it is again important that the feedback is understandable, helpful and actionable. Learners must listen to the feedback carefully, reflect and respond.

- It is vital to ensure that all learners have access to the feedback by using the appropriate technology.

31. Video Feedback

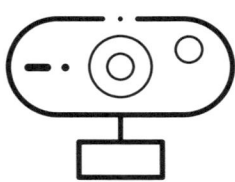 

How it works

As with the previous example, this is a method of feedback I used throughout the pandemic. It is important to add that I used this to provide whole-class feedback; I did not record separate videos for individual learners (as that would have proved difficult and demanding). Through video recordings I was able to give feedback, show examples, demonstrate techniques via modelling, and provide guidance and instruction. With this method students can view the feedback and, as with 'Audio Feedback', can press 'replay' if they want to revisit the feedback. I use a laptop to record feedback and upload videos to Google Classroom, but there are different variations as to how this can be achieved. As a department, we found it helpful to view the feedback videos as a form of reflection and sharing good practice. As head of department, this method informed me about the progress of students outside my classes.

Top tips

- If uploading feedback videos to YouTube, the content can be 'unlisted', so only learners with the link can access the recording. YouTube will show the number of views, but it will not show specifically who has (or hasn't) viewed the video.

- It can be easier and more sustainable to record individual video or audio feedback for learners in smaller class sizes, or to help specific learners who require additional support.
- Ensure the video clips are not too lengthy. Video clips should be short and snappy, clear and concise.

32. Peer Critique: Kind, Specific and Helpful – Ron Berger (2003)

Kind:
Kind critique is more effective and helps us to be more considerate.

Specific:
What exactly can your peer do, focus on or change to improve?

Helpful:
It's important to genuinely want to help make the work better, not just be critical.

How it works

The 'Kind, Specific and Helpful' approach to peer assessment and critique is taken from the work of celebrated author and educator Ron Berger, specifically from his book *An Ethic of Excellence: Building a Culture of Craftsmanship with Students* (2003). Berger points out that kindness is key, as feedback can be personal and emotive. It is important that while feedback is honest and constructive, it is communicated in a way that is not personal, mocking or insensitive but instead kind. Students do tend to give each other generalised or vague feedback, so specificity can help focus the feedback. Students need to recognise the value of peer assessment. The 'Kind, Specific and Helpful' approach is a great starting point. Further resources and support will be needed for peer assessment, such as mark schemes and/or success criteria.

Top tips

- 'Kind, Specific and Helpful' can be applied to and combined with any peer assessment task in this book.
- It can be useful to show students examples (and bad/non-examples) of feedback that are 'Kind, Specific and Helpful'.

- 'Kind, Specific and Helpful' feedback frames with sentence starters and prompts can be provided (see technique 38) to help students give good feedback to their peers.

33. Peer Critique: Listen, Reflect and Revise – Collaboration with Ron Berger

Listen: Listen carefully without being defensive. This is not critical of you, but aims to help you improve.

Reflect: Listening and reflection go hand in hand. What is the critique suggesting, and how is it helpful?

Revise: How can the critique and advice be actioned to improve the work and the learner?

How it works

I have had the privilege to interview Ron Berger (this episode is available via Teachers Talk Radio). After this discussion, I collaborated with Berger to further develop the 'Kind, Specific and Helpful' principles to include stages of response. If students ignore or disregard the feedback from their peer(s) (and fail to respond to it), even if it is kind, specific and helpful, then the feedback won't have an impact on progression. Therefore, when receiving critique from their peers, it is essential that students understand the importance of listening to or reading the peer feedback carefully. Afterwards, the student should take further time to think about the feedback. Finally, they should revise their work (once again emphasising the importance of actionable feedback with peer critique).

Top tips

- Being able to receive feedback well is essential. The principles do not just apply to peer assessment.
- To help students develop the habit of listening, reflecting and revising, specific time can be set aside for each stage.

- The listen/read, reflect and revise approach to feedback can be applied to any form of feedback, but it often needs to be emphasised and embedded with peer assessment.

34. Whole-Class Feedback Crib Sheets – Greg Thornton (2016)

What Went Well…	Even Better If…
Clear understanding and focus on the question shown by all. Good use of structure to answer questions with introduction, argument/counter argument and conclusion.	More specific and detailed examples were included to strengthen key points and arguments. Double check spelling of key terms such as dissolution, reformation, parliament and excommunication.
Questions for the class	**Next steps**
What was the role and significance of the people surrounding Henry VIII (key individuals) in terms of his decisions, actions and motivations?	Select a section of the exam essay to improve, assessing relevant examples and/or detail and correcting any literacy errors. Peer and self-assess revised answer.

How it works

This is a workload-friendly, effective and efficient method of providing whole-class feedback. The crib sheet resource, created by teacher and school leader Greg Thornton, was designed to support the teacher and students. When reviewing a class set of books, instead of the traditional method of adding written comments in each book, the teacher will record their thoughts and feedback on the crib sheet. During the following lesson, whole-class feedback can be communicated to the class while the crib sheet is referred to. This can hold learners to account, offering support and actionable feedback to move learning forwards. The crib sheet can include different sections that focus on areas of strength, areas for development, any causes for concern or individuals worthy of precise praise and so on.

Top tips

- A whole-class feedback crib sheet can be created to suit the context of the class.

- The teacher can use the information/feedback on the crib sheet to inform their lesson planning and to support responsive teaching, helping to decide the next steps.

- To see the original whole-class feedback crib sheet and find out more, visit the blog of Greg Thornton at https://mrthorntonteach.com/2016/04/08/marking-crib-sheet/.

35. Whole-Class Feedback: Live in the Lesson

How it works

This is a method I use in the lesson (in contrast to the crib sheet that is used when reviewing work outside of a lesson) to provide whole-class feedback (in-the-moment marking). When the class is working, I walk around the classroom and review their work. Instead of interrupting learners individually, I make notes. I then instruct all students to stop working and place their pens down to give me their full attention. I share my notes with the class, not naming names or pointing out individuals (although individual conversations can take place alongside this approach), but instead providing whole-class feedback based on my observations. Students then have to review their work and make any adjustments based on my whole-class feedback. This works particularly well when pointing out common mistakes, misconceptions or literacy errors without the teacher repeating the feedback to different learners.

> **Top tips**
>
> - I use a clipboard or notebook, but notes can also be recorded digitally. I do this to create a record of the key points I want to share with the class.
> - The observations taken during the lesson can support adaptive teaching as the teacher can make a record of students who require further support or challenge.

36. Student-Friendly Mark Schemes

What the exam board says...	What the exam board means...	What this means for me...

How it works

For several years I was an external examiner. I attended annual compulsory training where the mark scheme was discussed and explained thoroughly. It is important to remember mark schemes are not designed for students and they are not created to help teachers. The purpose of an exam mark scheme is to support examiners and moderators. However, mark schemes are accessible online, and it can be helpful for students to be familiar with and understand the language and requirements of the mark scheme. Phrasing and terminology used in official mark schemes can be difficult for students to grasp, but creating a student-friendly version (without any jargon) can help students understand and engage with feedback in an accessible, practical and actionable way. I saw an example of this in a GCSE English lesson at King's High Warwick. I spoke to several students in the English lesson, and I was incredibly impressed with their very secure knowledge and understanding of the mark scheme. They said that the resource, created by the teacher, had helped them immensely.

Top tips

- Some exam boards and websites create student-style mark schemes that can be downloaded to use.
- Student-friendly mark schemes can be used for peer and self-assessment.
- It is important to regularly check for student understanding when using any mark scheme.
- The 'curse of knowledge' is a cognitive bias, where an individual assumes others share the same level of knowledge, understanding and expertise as they do. It is useful for teachers to be aware of this cognitive bias when providing feedback to learners and using mark schemes.

37. Exam Wrappers – Marsha Lovett (2013)

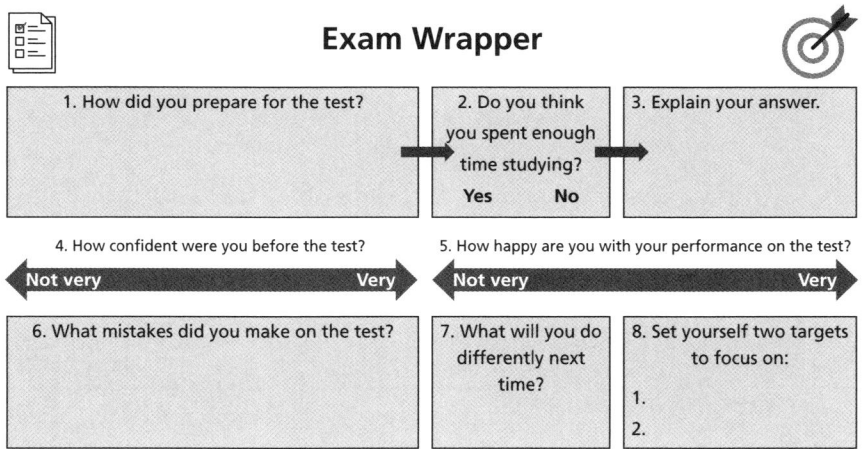

How it works

'Exam Wrappers' were designed as a post-assessment self-reflection resource for graduate students. It has since been adapted and used across different subjects and ages within school settings. The example above was created by secondary biology teacher and research lead Louise Lewis. Following an assessment, it can be tempting for students to focus on scores and grades, but they must engage with and reflect upon the feedback provided in order to help them learn and continue to progress. 'Exam Wrappers' encourage all students to reflect (openly and honestly) on their effort and preparation prior to the exam. They also provide students with the opportunity to record their mistakes and areas of development. To complete this 'Exam Wrapper', a student must carefully go through the questions and record mistakes and set targets to inform their next steps.

Top tips

- A generic template, as shown above, can be used and shared across a body of staff. Subject-specific versions can be created.
- The template can be used as a prompt for reflective conversations among learners.

38. Peer Assessment Feedback Frames – Durrington Research School

Kind
- I really like the way you _____
- Excellent _____ throughout
- The most successful thing about this was _____
- I enjoyed reading this because _____
- It was especially good when you _____

Specific
- In the first/second/third paragraph…
- I think _____ needs more focus on/could include more connotation/could include more media terminology etc.
- Your sentence/paragraph about _____ was _____ because _____

Helpful (refer to success criteria)
- You need to add _____
- Don't forget to _____
- To improve your _____ try _____
- Perhaps you could …

How it works

I am a fan and follower of the Durrington Research School blog. There are many useful and practical blog posts written by different staff members. The example above was shared on the blog, and a link to the website can be found at the back of this book (Class Teaching, 2015). This framework provides sentence starters and guidance for students based on the Ron Berger 'Kind, Specific and Helpful' principles of peer assessment (see feedback technique 32). Students can use the examples from the feedback frame when providing verbal or written peer feedback. This helps to ensure the feedback is meaningful (not generic or vague). Students can be given a copy of the feedback frame (a paper or digital version) to regularly refer to when conducting peer assessment.

> **Top tips**
>
> - This is a form of scaffolding with the goal being to remove the feedback frames when students develop the skills and confidence to provide kind, specific, helpful and actionable feedback.
> - I have used this with younger learners, but it can be adapted for older students/exam classes.

39. Two Stars and a Wish (Peer Assessment)

How it works

'Two Stars and a Wish' is a very well-known and widely used feedback technique. The concept is clear and simple as two areas of strength are identified (as stars) followed by one target (a wish). This is a student-friendly format, and it can be used as an opportunity to provide 'Precise Praise' (see technique 27) in addition to actionable feedback with a target in mind. A problem (and in my opinion, a significant one!) is the time it can take for a teacher to provide 'Two Stars and a Wish' for every learner in their class. For example, I used this technique with my key stage three classes only (excluding GCSE and A-level) with three written comments per student. The workload was 540 written comments in one week! This is not workload friendly, sustainable or arguably the best use of teacher time. However, as a method of peer assessment, where students are required to give 'Two Stars and a Wish' to their partner, this can potentially be a structured, efficient and effective method of providing peer feedback. It is a much more manageable technique for students than it is for teachers.

Top tips

- It is important to demonstrate good examples of 'Precise Praise' to students, so that they can avoid simply giving generic or oversimplified praise to their partner. Ron Berger (2003) advises teachers and students to focus on accomplishments, not compliments.
- Learners should ensure the 'wish' is an actionable task that is relevant to the work and supports the learner to make progress overall.
- There are various templates available online for this feedback technique.

40. The ABC Model

Agree with	From the response your partner gave, what point(s) do you agree with and why?
Build upon	After reading/listening to your partner's answers, how can you build upon it by adding more information or relevant examples?
Challenge	Is there anything that you disagree with or you do not think is correct? You must explain your reasons and remember to challenge in a kind, specific and helpful manner.

How it works

This is a questioning technique used by teachers to encourage debate and discussion among learners in pairs, in groups or during whole-class discussions. Students use the 'ABC Model' to provide feedback about their initial responses. The 'ABC Model' naturally works best for open-ended answers where there is the possibility for agreement, disagreement, examples and counterexamples in contrast to a short, closed question (although it is possible to use the 'ABC Model' with shorter responses). A central element of the 'ABC Model' is the opportunity for elaboration and to develop oracy skills. It is not enough for students to agree or disagree; they must explore this and explain their reasons for doing so with supporting arguments and evidence.

Top tips

- The responses using the 'ABC Model' can be verbal or written, or both. The 'ABC model' works well with other classroom techniques such as 'Think-Pair-Share'.
- Sentence starters could be provided for each section of the model, with examples modelled to the class to show the 'ABC Model' in action.

41. Think-Pair-Share (TPS) – Frank Lyman (1981)

How it works

'Think-Pair-Share' (TPS) is a commonly used and well-established classroom technique. Students are provided with a question, statement or problem to solve. They should be allowed individual thinking time, followed by time to discuss their response and thoughts with a partner. The final stage involves sharing and discussing answers at a whole-class level. This technique can be used to develop a wide range of skills, including oracy and feedback – central elements of TPS. During the pair stage, learners give each other feedback, and in the final share stage, the teacher can provide feedback to individuals, pairs and/or the whole class. Students need to realise that the pair stage is an opportunity to share, reflect, discuss and provide one another with feedback (in contrast to a social chat).

Top tips

- The pair section can be carefully structured to ensure both students can contribute (and ensure the conversation is not dominated by one student or allowing a student to opt out). Students can be assigned numbers so that when the teacher instructs the number 1 students to talk, number 2 students must listen. They then switch when the teacher signals to do so.
- Students can provide feedback reciprocally using the 'ABC Model' (see the previous technique).
- Mini-whiteboards can be used to record student responses, and students can easily amend their answers during the pair stage if they wish to do so based on the feedback they have received.

42. Read, Reflect, Check, Correct

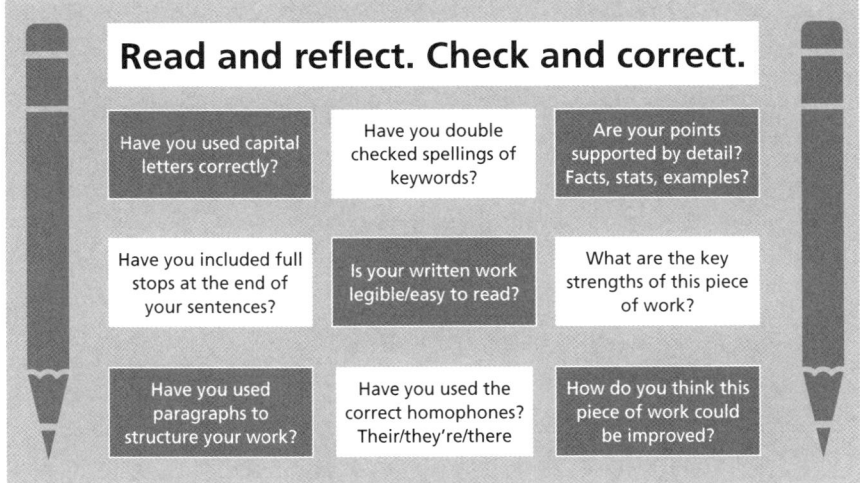

How it works

I created this resource to encourage my students to develop the habit of regular review, reflection, checking and correcting. The resource can be adapted for different ages and across different subjects. The example above has a focus on literacy. It could be used for peer and/or self-assessment. Rather than asking or instructing students to check their work, this resource provides specific instructions and guidance for learners when reading through their classwork. This can act as pre-emptive feedback: instead of the teacher identifying mistakes/errors when work is submitted, the student can find and fix them prior to submission to the teacher.

> **Top tips**
>
> - Students can refer to a paper copy of the resource or a digital version on a virtual learning platform.
> - The resource can be adapted for specific tasks. For example, it can have a focus on success criteria or exam question requirements.

43. Gallery Critique – Ron Berger

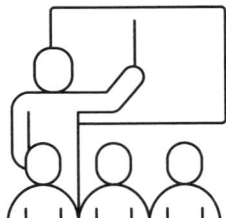 

How it works

This is a peer assessment task where students receive feedback from several of their peers (in contrast to one or two). Student work will be on display and time will be needed for learners to view different pieces of work. This work could be a painting, illustration or model, an answer to an exam question, or a section of a piece of creative writing. It is essential that students have access to success criteria and/or a mark scheme to ensure the feedback provided is linked to the task and learning intentions. In addition to being kind, specific and helpful, the feedback should also be understandable and actionable (students can write their feedback on a Post-it note or on a feedback sheet). When students return to their classwork, they will need time to read, reflect on and action the feedback from their peers.

Top tips:
- The work can be anonymised to reduce or remove any potential bias (although students can sometimes recognise their peers' work).

- I usually advise students to review four or five different pieces of work, but this will depend on a range of variables, so the teacher should use their professional judgement to decide how long to spend on the task and how to instruct the class. The students receiving the feedback could be overwhelmed with multiple targets or pieces of advice, so they can select one specific area to focus on and implement.

- This task requires careful planning and specific guidance and instructions. For example, students can be assigned pieces of work to review (in contrast to students randomly selecting, which could lead to some students receiving more (or less) feedback than others!).

44. Flashcards

How it works

'Flashcards' are a very versatile teaching and learning resource that can be used inside and outside the classroom. They can be used with younger students learning new words or for quizzing, with questions and answers on alternate sides. Another idea is to include key terms on one side and definitions or translations on the other side. Flashcards can provide instant feedback to learners as the correct answers can be seen on the reverse side of the card. Students can also use them to self-assess and revise through self-quizzing. They can also be used with peers for paired quizzing. Furthermore, parents can use flashcards to quiz their child and check for accuracy. The feedback element is essential to ensuring flashcards are used effectively, to strengthen recall, and to identify and close gaps in knowledge.

Top tips

- Flashcards can be paper or digital in format. There are pros and cons to each.
- Flashcards don't need to be flashy, but simple, clear and explicitly linked to curriculum content.
- Students need to be shown how to use flashcards correctly. Older students can be taught to create their own..

- Students should revisit flashcards until they have been mastered, where students can answer quickly, confidently and correctly.
- To space out the use of flashcards and revisit gaps in knowledge, the 'Leitner System' can be used (see the next technique).

45. The Leitner System – Sebastian Leitner

How it works

It is essential that flashcards are not used as a last-minute revision strategy by students. A way to overcome this and to support organisation and commitment to revisiting flashcards is known as the 'Leitner System', named after Sebastian Leitner who developed this method in the 1970s. The aim is to help students revisit the cards/topics that they have previously struggled with, until they can retrieve that information with ease and confidence. On a Monday, students should attempt to answer the questions on the flashcards. The flashcards will then be allocated to different boxes, depending on whether they were answered correctly or not. If the student answers correctly, the flashcard will go in the box labelled 'Box two: Tuesday and Thursday', meaning they will return to the flashcard on those days. If the student cannot answer the question or provides an incorrect answer, they put the flashcard in box one, the 'Everyday box' (revisiting the flashcard each day to support the retrieval process). The following day, students will repeat the process. If they can still not answer the flashcards from box one, they remain there, but each flashcard mastered will move to box two. If students answer a question from box two incorrectly then it goes back to box one. When students are able to correctly answer the questions in box two, they will be moved to box three: only to be revisited on Friday. This process will be repeated, either with the same flashcards or varied for different subjects and topics.

Top tips

- There is an excellent explanation of the 'Leitner System' by teacher Jon Hutchinson on YouTube. In this video clip, Jon shares how his primary class created flashcards and used the 'Leitner System' for regular self-quizzing and self-checking.

46. Moderation Marking

How it works

'Moderation Marking' involves more than one teacher reviewing and assessing students' work. It can help to ensure that feedback (in the form of comments, grades or scores) is consistent, valid, reliable and fair. 'Moderation Marking' can be completed across a department, phase, multi-academy trust (MAT) or with external moderators to assess the judgements made. 'Moderation Marking' can also act as a form of professional learning and development, helping teachers to gain further in-depth understanding of the mark scheme and criteria (this can be very beneficial for early career teachers or non-specialists). 'Moderation Marking' can potentially help teachers to identify trends and common mistakes across a sample of learners. There are many benefits to moderation, but it does require more time than individual marking as teachers will need to read, reflect on and discuss their individual feedback and reach an agreement. 'Moderation Marking' is often more relevant to some subjects over others. For example, it can be very helpful in English, humanities and subjects that require students to write extended answers or essays.

Top tips

- Leaders should plan and assign time on the calendar for staff to meet to moderate. It is important to do so at a time that does not interfere with other commitments; for example, parents' evening or as a report deadline is approaching.
- Moderators should aim to review and moderate a wide range of samples. This can include samples from different classes and from a mix of genders and grades.
- To gain further experience of moderating formally assessed work, teachers could become external examiners.

47. Comparative Judgement

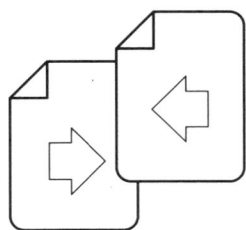

How it works

In recent years, this approach to assessment and feedback has gathered a lot of interest. To simplify, 'Comparative Judgement' requires the teacher (or moderator) to review a pair of student responses or essays side by side, and judge which they think is better. This process is repeated, and student work is then ranked based on overall quality (marks can then be assigned). It can be easier and quicker for teachers to make direct comparisons, in contrast to overall individual judgements. This can be completed by individual teachers or as part of 'Moderation Marking' (see previous technique). Daisy Christodoulou, director of education at No More Marking (an online comparative judgement platform), explains, 'The judgement they make is a holistic one about the overall quality of the writing. It is not guided by a rubric and can be completed fairly quickly. If each marker makes a series of such judgements, it is possible for an algorithm to combine all the judgements and use them to construct a measurement scale' (researchED, 2018).

Top tips

- This approach naturally lends itself well to subjects such as English and humanities, but it can also be used in practical and performance-based subjects. It can also be used across ages and key stages.
- To find out more about 'Comparative Judgement', I recommend visiting the website nomoremarking.com and reading the blogs of Daisy Christodoulou.

48. Hangman Spellings

Parlement　　　*Parl _ _ ment*
Sp

How it works

This was a literacy approach that all staff were instructed to use at the first school I taught at, Elfed High School in Buckley, North Wales. Not every spelling error would be identified as a 'Hangman Spelling' (the two main reasons were teacher workload and students could be overwhelmed if there were a lot of spelling errors highlighted). The teacher uses their professional judgement to be selective. The premise is simple: a spelling mistake is identified (often with a missing letter or mistaken letter order) with a literacy code, and the hangman approach helps the learner to identify the error in the word. The correct letters remain, as shown in the example above with the word 'Parliament'. A literacy code will highlight a spelling error but not show the student specifically where the error is, although they can use a word list or knowledge organiser to find out. This is a quick actionable feedback task and spelling strategy. The students must complete the spelling in order to have a record of the correct spelling. This can be carried out in a lesson with live/in-the-moment marking. This can also be used with peer assessment, but it is essential the students are correctly identifying a spelling mistake and that the corrected spelling is accurate to avoid any confusion.

> **Top tips**
>
> - This technique was referred to as 'Hangman Spellings' in the school I worked at because it looks like the popular guessing game 'Hangman'. However, another name could be used such as 'Fill in the Blanks', especially as the term 'hangman' could potentially be triggering. This is sometimes referred to as 'Spaceman Spellings' because the students must fill in the spaces to complete the word.

- Students should be encouraged to double check the accuracy of spellings using a word list, glossary, knowledge organiser or dictionary.
- It is important to be selective and not highlight too many spelling errors.

49. Progression Not Perfection

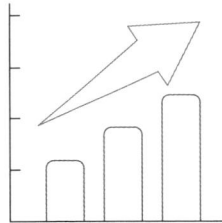

How it works

This is not a feedback technique, but instead a well-known feedback principle for students to be aware of and apply to their studies. Some students can strive for perfection and become frustrated at not achieving this, even if they have made progress. The 'Progression Not Perfection' attitude encourages students to recognise and focus on the smaller but significant achievements in their learning journey. The process of regularly identifying progress – via teacher, peer or self-feedback – can increase student confidence, self-esteem and motivation. By contrast, constantly focusing on gaps in knowledge or the failure to achieve perfection can be demoralising. This links with growth mindset, which involves making marginal gains and becoming resilient, as mistakes are a normal and natural part of the learning process. Setting manageable and realistic goals can also help students to focus on progress over perfection.

Top tips

- The principle of 'Progression Not Perfection' can apply to many different fields, such as sport, nutrition and business to name a few. Explaining this to students can help them to grasp the concept.

- The 'Tick Trick' by Adam Boxer (see technique 70) can also help students to value correct aspects of an answer, even if they do make a mistake.

50. Modelling

How it works

'Modelling' can serve a range of different purposes in the classroom, including a method of providing feedback to learners. It can help students to understand expectations and how they can improve. It is important that students understand the concept of modelling as a form of demonstration, in contrast to copying or replicating what the teacher does. Providing feedback such as 'add more detail' or 'include relevant statistics to support your argument', can be supported by specific examples shared by the teacher to help students understand what they need to do next and what success looks like. Various teaching techniques include modelling, such as worked examples, 'I do, We do, You do' and the use of a visualiser.

> **Top tips**
> - 'Modelling' can be used as a method of pre-emptive feedback to address common misconceptions and mistakes upfront, to prevent students from making those mistakes.

- 'Modelling' can be used as a feedback technique throughout the learning process. With chunking, for example, the teacher can model how to write and structure an introduction, which can be followed by students attempting to do so independently. This can be followed by further modelling with the students attempting the body of an essay. Finally, the teacher can model how a judgement is reached, sustained and explained in a conclusion. Following this process, the students can apply the skills and knowledge learned to structure different answers and essays.

51. Tell Me More! (Elaborate and Extend)

A sole trader is a type of business.	A sole trader is a type of business owned and operated by one person. They have full control and keep all profits, but they also have unlimited liability.
A strong brand helps a business stand out from competitors.	A strong brand helps a business to stand out from its competitors. This can lead to or increase customer loyalty and allow the business to charge premium prices, and therefore be more profitable and successful.
A stakeholder is any person or group with an interest in a business.	A stakeholder is any person or group with an interest in a business or organisation, such as employees, customers or suppliers. In a school setting, stakeholders include staff, students, parents, governors and the local community.

How it works

I have used this method as an opportunity for retrieval practice, as students recall information from long-term memory by building on a prompt or their initial response. I would often find myself writing feedback to students focusing on adding more depth and detail, but instead of providing this feedback to multiple students repeatedly, it can be presented to the whole class. It can also be a way to ensure that feedback focused on adding more detail to answers and classwork is an actionable, concrete task. The example above shows a GCSE business student response in the first column, while the second column shows where they have elaborated on and extended their original point, adding more specific detail and examples. It is important for students to recognise that this feedback is about improving the individual, not the work, meaning it should be something they transfer and apply to all relevant contexts, not just a single piece of work.

Top tips

- This feedback technique can be combined with other techniques in this book, including 'Yellow Box Method' (technique 23) or 'Editing Tabs' (technique 29).

52. Self-Assessment with Quizzing

Do Now Activity: Check your answers

Q1. What is a fuel? *A substance that releases the stored energy when it is burned.*
Q2. What unit do we use to measure energy? *Joules, J.*
Q3. What is an energy store? *When energy is held by an object for a time.*
Q4. Which energy store is involved in fuels, food and batteries? *Chemical energy store.*
Q5. Which energy store is involved when objects heat up or cool down? *Thermal energy store.*
Q6. How is energy moved between energy stores? *By energy transfer.*
Q7. What is the law of conservation of energy? *Energy cannot be created or destroyed.*
Q8. Which energy transfer is often involved in changing the temperature of objects? *Transfer from hot to cold.*

How it works

A 'Do Now' task (created by Doug Lemov in *Teach Like a Champion 3.0*, 2021) is a way to ensure learners are engaged, focused and on task at the beginning of a lesson. It can be a great opportunity for regular retrieval practice, as shown in the science example above. There are many ways to provide feedback with quizzing, but it is important to remember that retrieval practice should be low stakes. Peer assessment for some learners could create a high-stakes or stressful learning environment. I would advise the teacher to provide whole-class feedback to the 'Do Now' questions and allow students to self-assess, so they can see for themselves what they do and don't know (this is also low stakes). The questions above are taken from *Springboard KS3 Science Knowledge Book* (2024), authored by Claudia Allan, Jovita Castelino, Thomas Millichamp, Adam Robbins and Bill Wilkinson, and the series editor is Adam Boxer.

Top tips

- This method of self-assessment can be combined with 'Correct or Consolidate' (technique 19) and/or 'Retrieval Reflection Ticket' (technique 20) and potentially 'Tick Trick' (technique 70) depending on the questions asked.

53. Success Criteria

Year 4 English – Narrative Writing Success Criteria
I can ... Organise writing into paragraphs Use a range of conjunctions to link ideas Include speech punctuation in dialogue (e.g. What are you doing?) Use fronted adverbials (e.g. As the sun rose, ...) Expand noun phrases with adjectives (e.g. fierce tiger) Write in the third person (e.g. She ran through the grass) Choose pronouns and nouns appropriately to avoid repetition

How it works

Success criteria are descriptions of the desired performance in learning tasks and the manageable breakdown of the learning intentions to help students achieve the desired goal in terms of content, skills and/or knowledge to be learned. These criteria can be used as part of peer and/or self-assessment and for teacher feedback. They allow learners to monitor their own progress and evaluate their success. These criteria can also show students explicitly what success looks like. There can be generic success criteria for written-based class tasks to act as a reminder to learners to focus on literacy skills, or the criteria could be more subject specific, as shown with the example above. Time should be spent discussing and explaining the success criteria so that students can use it appropriately.

Top tips

- Success criteria, where possible, should be shared with students for them to refer to during different stages of the learning process (not just after task completion), encouraging independence and reflection with ongoing self-checking and correcting.

- It is important that success criteria do not become 'lethally mutated' as tick boxes or a checklist that is glued in books and not engaged with. Success criteria should support learners to make progress and understand how to be successful.

54. TAG Me

T – Tell me something you like (about my work)

A – Ask me a question (based on the work)

G – Give me a suggestion (to improve my work)

How it works

This is a very straightforward method of peer assessment. The first point, **'Tell me something you like'** is to encourage learners to provide precise praise to their peers. **'Ask me a question'** is an opportunity for a student to find out more, encouraging their partner to explain further and expand on their original points or answer. The final point, **'Give me a suggestion'**, is the part of the peer assessment that should be actionable. The suggestion should have an instruction or guidance as to how their peer(s) can develop and improve their work. This should help the learner understand what their next steps are. This could be used to support verbal or written peer feedback. As with all peer assessment techniques, to ensure the feedback is not generic and vague, support in the form of success criteria, a mark scheme or peer prompts should be provided.

Top tips

- The 'TAG Me' comments can be written on a Post-it note or mini-whiteboard to record the feedback without writing on student work.
- This feedback technique could be combined with 'Gallery Critique' (see technique 43).
- Feedback frames and sentence starters can be provided to further support learners.
- There are videos of the 'TAG Me' feedback technique available to view on YouTube, including videos filmed in the classroom.

55. SPaG Watch/ Literacy Leaders

How it works

This technique focuses on spelling, punctuation and grammar (SPaG). 'SPaG Watch' involves assigning students to a role where their responsibility is to review their classmates' work (when instructed to do so by the teacher) and provide focused feedback. For my younger classes, students were assigned specific roles such as Punctuation Police, and they were tasked with checking that capital letters and full stops were used accurately (I have observed a primary lesson where an individual was assigned the role of Captain Capital Letters with the sole purpose to check for the correct use of capital letters). The Spelling Squad were responsible for providing feedback on spellings. For older students, I have adapted the concept to 'Literacy Leaders' where two or more students circulate the class to check literacy. In my experience, students responded well to this. When learners knew their peers would be checking for literacy accuracy, they dedicated careful attention to literacy details. The students carrying out the SPaG watch/literacy leader's role could also be given resources, such as a word list, to ensure they are providing accurate feedback to their peers.

Top tips

- Students can be given a lanyard or badge to wear to identify them as the 'SPaG Watch'.
- The teacher can select individuals to take on the roles, but selection should not just be limited to the learners that are regarded as 'gifted and talented'. Instead, all learners should be given the opportunity to provide feedback to their peers.
- Feedback can be verbal, or students could use literacy codes and/or 'Hangman Spellings' (technique 48).

56. It Takes Two

How it works

This is a form of peer assessment carried out in pairs. Each pair in the class will give their work to another pair. Two (or more) students will review a piece of classwork by their peers. They must discuss the work, referring to the success criteria/mark scheme and reach an agreement about the feedback they will provide. This dialogue helps learners to reflect upon and verbalise their thoughts and feedback. Their partner may agree or could challenge the feedback. The pairs then review the work of the second individual (again with a feedback-focused conversation) and do the same. Once the pairs have reviewed both pieces of classwork, they each meet with a member of the second pair to explain and share the feedback and listen to the feedback decided upon by the other pair of learners. The student receiving the feedback knows it is from two people, not just one individual.

Top tips

- This can take place during or after a piece of work has been completed. This task takes longer than peer feedback in pairs as students require time to discuss and reach a conclusion.

- During the feedback conversations, students can record the feedback they will give. This can be written on a Post-it note, mini-whiteboard or in the margin of the class book.

- The principles of 'Kind, Specific and Helpful' apply when students are discussing the feedback and communicating it to their peers.
- This approach can be combined with the 'ABC Model' (technique 40).

57. Visualisers

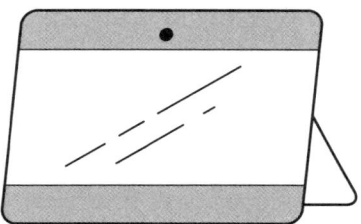

How it works

Visualisers can be used in many ways to support feedback in the classroom. A visualiser is a digital camera that reflects images onto the screen in the classroom. It is a simple but versatile device, suitable for every classroom. It can be used for modelling, reading through answers with a class, drafting responses and providing whole-class feedback. A visualiser can be used to share and discuss success criteria and mark schemes. Another useful way to use a visualiser is to annotate student responses or a teacher-generated example. By sharing an example answer using a visualiser, a teacher can show a class how a mark scheme can be assigned to a response (and highlight what is missing), or the teacher can ask the class to give collective feedback on a piece of work. A visualiser could be used to identify misconceptions and common mistakes, and to model how to give feedback. It can provide in-the-lesson, real-time feedback for students to work on.

> **Top tips**
>
> - An alternative to a visualiser is the mirroring function on tablet devices that can also be used to project an image from an iPad or iPhone camera onto the screen. If you don't use a visualiser in the classroom, I encourage you to do so – it can be a powerful tool in the teaching and learning toolkit. Apps like CamScanner and Microsoft Lens enable users to take high-quality photos of classwork to convert to PDF or project on screen through sharing via email or transfer.
> - Most visualisers allow the teacher to screen record or save annotations so that they can be used for future use or revisited later.

58. 'The Feedback Sandwich'

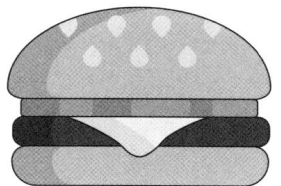

> The presentation of the dish was excellent. The bright and vibrant colours looked great and it made the food look appetising. An area to improve would be to add seasoning as this could enhance the overall taste with more flavour. The portion size was perfect, not too much or too little but just right!

How it works

The aim of 'The Feedback Sandwich' is to provide a combination of positive and constructive comments with the targets and areas for development sandwiched between two pieces of positive feedback or praise. This type of feedback is not suitable for the teacher to provide for every individual in the class, as it will require too much time, energy and effort, but like the 'Two Stars and a Wish' technique, it can be a helpful way to develop peer-assessment skills. The example above shows peer feedback given in a food and nutrition lesson. The student gives their partner a positive comment, followed by a target and actionable advice, followed by more positive and precise praise. In this context, the student has finished the task (as their dish was cooked) but the actionable feedback (to add more seasoning) could be applied in the future. Therefore, it can be useful for the student to record this feedback to refer to and apply in the next practical lesson.

Top tips

- I think this feedback model can be a useful starting point for peer assessment, but it is basic and can be restrictive. Students should eventually move beyond this method once they have developed the skills and experience of providing feedback to one another.

- Other feedback techniques can be combined with 'The Feedback Sandwich'. For example, 'Kind, Specific and Helpful' (technique 32) and 'Precise Praise Postcards' (technique 28).
- This can be a verbal and/or written form of peer assessment and feedback.

59. Feedback Journal

How it works

This is another self-explanatory feedback technique, as students are instructed to record their feedback in a journal or in their school planner. Not every piece of feedback should be included in the journal – there isn't always time, and indeed this might not always be the best use of student time. However, recording feedback can help the learner to engage, reflect on and act upon that feedback. In secondary schools, for example, the English teacher does not know what feedback the student is receiving from their history teacher and vice versa. The teachers could be giving the student similar (or identical) feedback, and they may both be unaware of this. The only person who knows all the feedback they receive is the student. By recording it, the learner can apply and transfer the relevant feedback. The journal can also record student progress. As they make progress, the feedback they receive will change and develop. A journal can help to ensure the feedback provided is memorable, and even if students forget the feedback from the last lesson, last week or last term, they still have a record to which they can refer. This is a great resource to complement and support the 'Flashback Feedback' method (technique 17).

Top tips

- A variation of this can be writing a reflective letter. The letter could be to a teacher, peer or family member. The focus of this method is for students to share their successes and areas for development. Another idea could be a 'letter to my future self', where learners write to their future selves to provide advice, guidance and actionable targets. The letters can be revisited and reviewed.

60. Student Sampling

How it works

History teacher Derrick Roberts has found this approach to be very effective, supporting his workload and his students' progress. Roberts explained the method in a case study featured in *Feedback: Strategies to Support Teacher Workload and Improve Pupil Progress* (2024): 'The process is very simple. I select a number of books, between a quarter and a third, from each class and mark them really well, following the school's policy, looking for positives and misconceptions. I then record the findings on a crib sheet. This crib sheet has sections where I record the common misconceptions, literacy errors and examples of what they did well. I also record for my own information any students who are giving me cause for concern and I make sure that I find time for individual conversations with these students.' The teacher could keep a record of the students' books they have reviewed to ensure that next time different students are selected in the sample. A concern could be raised about students not being selected, but the teacher has other ways in which they can monitor and provide feedback to all learners in the class.

> **Top tips**
> - There are variations of this technique. One approach can include writing comments in selected class books, whereas another includes reviewing a sample of books (or essays, answers, folders, etc.) and not including any written feedback, but instead making a note using a whole-class feedback crib sheet.

- 'Student Sampling' can also be used with 'Moderation Marking' (technique 46). Moderation can take time as staff will share and discuss the decisions and feedback. It is more viable, therefore, to select a sample in contrast to moderating every answer or book.

61. Emoji Exit Ticket

Emoji Exit Ticker
Circle the emoji(s) that reflect how you got on today in the lesson. Explain your reasons why...

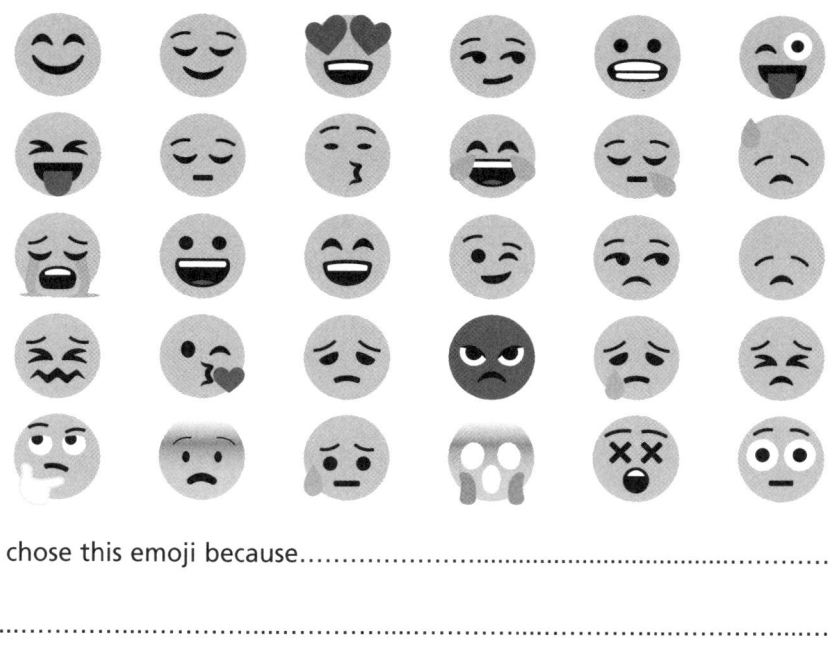

I chose this emoji because..

....

....

How it works

This is a self-reflection exit ticket (Jones, 2018) that was designed as an opportunity for students to consider how they are feeling regarding their progress and about school in general. This is a pastoral exit ticket, in contrast to an academic task to check for understanding. I have used this with younger learners, together with regular conversations and questions to discover how I can further support their learning and progress. It is a quick and simple task where students select emojis to represent how they are feeling and/or their level of confidence. They must explain the reasons for selecting the emojis. Through this exit ticket, I have discovered students have struggled or lacked confidence, which I had not picked up on for various reasons. It can be lovely to read positive comments from students about enjoying lessons or the subject content. Student reflections can be influenced by factors that don't necessarily demonstrate a self-awareness of their level of understanding or progress. For example, a student could select happy emoji faces because they found the lesson interesting, but this doesn't guarantee they understood the lesson content (that also must be explicitly checked).

Top tips

- Younger learners can select the emoji and explain the reasons for doing so verbally to their partner or the teacher.
- This resource can be adapted for older students as an opportunity to reflect on their levels of confidence and/or overall wellbeing.

62. Visual Mark Schemes

GCSE DANCE PE

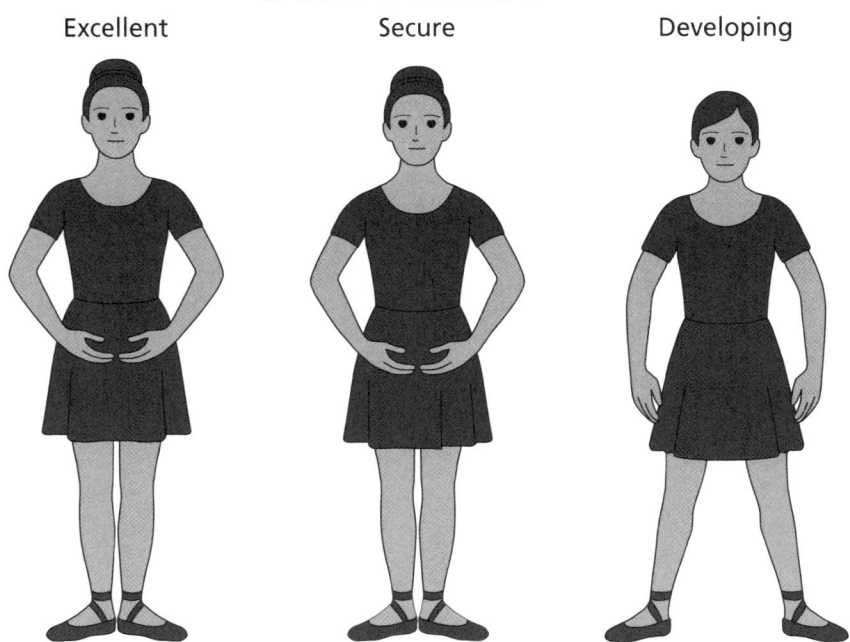

How it works

If sharing mark schemes with students, they must be student friendly. For practical subjects, a 'Visual Mark Scheme' can be very helpful. The example above focuses on GCSE dance with the first position in ballet shown as 'developing' (as the positions of the legs are not accurate), 'secure' (the shoulders are slightly lowered) and 'excellent'. This can prompt discussion and questions (for example, explaining the difference between the 'excellent' and 'developing' example). 'Visual Mark Schemes' can support younger learners, students with SEND and EAL learners.

They can also include shapes, illustrations, photos, diagrams, graphs and more. Students can refer to them for peer and/or self-assessment. Students could be tasked to create their own 'Visual Mark Schemes' with photos of themselves, found examples or illustrations.

> **Top tips**
>
> - The images must be carefully selected as they must be relevant to the content. Royalty- and copyright-free images can be downloaded from websites such as Pixabay.com or Unsplash.com, and icons can be selected and used from the website nounproject.com. AI can be used to generate 'Visual Mark Schemes' to support students.
> - QR codes can also be included on mark schemes with links to video clips, resources and support.

63. Progress Photos

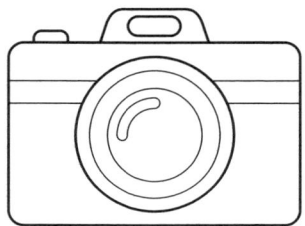 

How it works

I have viewed 'Progress Photos' in a wide range of classroom contexts ranging from EYFS to GCSE product design. EYFS practitioners regularly take photos to record student progress and share it with parents. Older learners can take photos of their work without the support of the teacher and keep a digital or printed portfolio of their progress. 'Progress Photos' can be useful for reflection, as students can review what they have completed previously and use the photos to inform their progress and decide on next steps. Once a task or project has been completed, the photos taken throughout the process should be a record of what the student has achieved. 'Progress Photos' can also be used within practical subjects; for example, in PE to provide feedback on body position and technique.

> ### Top tips
> - 'Progress Photos' can be used as visual and verbal prompts; for example, asking students questions about the learning and feedback, such as 'Can you explain what you are doing in this photo and how it is linked to your learning?'

- General Data Protection Regulation (GDPR) is a data protection law within the European Union (passed into UK law) that is specifically focused on how organisations (including schools) collect, store and use personal data. This applies to all staff, and children of course also have the same rights as adults under GDPR law. Photographs are considered personal data; therefore, transparency and consent are required when taking and sharing photos of students and their work. To find out more about GDPR, visit www.gov.uk/guidance/data-protection-in-schools.

64. STAR Feedback

Strengths	Key strengths identified by the peer or teacher.
Target	A suggested target to focus on for improvement.
Action	Linked to the target; a specific action to be taken by the student.
Respond	Teacher responds to the completed action by the student.

How it works

I have observed many school contexts using the 'STAR Feedback' method, across different ages, key stages and subjects. I personally like this approach because of the specific focus given to acting on feedback, which is often a missing piece of the feedback puzzle. As with all feedback techniques and strategies, it is for the classroom teachers and leaders to use their professional knowledge, expertise and judgement in deciding how to implement this. 'STAR Feedback' does not have to be restricted to written comments. There is the potential for this type of feedback to steer into 'triple marking' territory with teacher feedback, student action and further teacher feedback – this is not workload friendly or sustainable. 'STAR Feedback' can also be used for whole-class feedback, and learners can use this with peer assessment to structure the feedback they give.

Top tips

- This can be combined with many of the feedback techniques described throughout this book, such as the selective marking approaches (with 'Successful Snapshots' to address the strength and 'Yellow Box Method' to identify the target/action).
- A goal for students could be to ensure the target becomes an area of strength in the future through action and response.

65. Read Aloud and Reflect

How it works

The many benefits of reading aloud have been explored through research and widely discussed in education. Reading aloud can support younger learners and EAL students, and help to develop a wide range of oracy skills through speaking and listening, with learning to talk and learning through talk. There are several feedback techniques throughout this book that provide opportunities for learners to provide verbal feedback to their peers, engage in meaningful dialogue with their teacher and verbally reflect on their progress. In 2024, the Oracy Education Commission published 'We need to talk: The report of the Commission on the Future of Oracy Education in England'. The report stated:

> 'The promise of oracy education is far-reaching. Oral language and communication skills can enhance well-being, improve employability and foster improved civic engagement.' The report added, 'We believe that oracy is as foundational in learning as reading, writing and arithmetic. It should be an entitlement in every child's education to prepare them as future citizens.'

Reading work out loud (their own and that of their peer) can help students to recognise and rectify mistakes they have made. Students can be instructed to read short answers or paragraphs to a peer, and in doing so, the focus can move away from spellings and towards content.

Through reading aloud, students can often identify where punctuation and grammar conventions are missing, if words are repeated or if the flow of a sentence needs changing.

> **Top tips**
> - If students are reading their work aloud to their partner, they should be encouraged to talk clearly and slowly. Responses should be read aloud through chunking, one answer or sentence at a time (depending on the age and context of the learners).

66. Feedback Acronyms

DIRT – Dedicated Improvement Reflection Time	**WWW** – What Went Well **EBI** – Even Better If	**SPaG** – Spelling, Punctuation and Grammar
NS – Next Steps	**CRAFT** – Clear, Relevant, Actionable, Focused, Timely	**STAR** – Strengths, Target, Action, Respond
AO – Assessment Objectives	**WAGOLL** – What a Good One Looks Like	**WABOLL** – What a Bad One Looks Like
TAG Me – Tell me, Ask me and Give me	**HTI/TTI** – How to Improve/ Try This Instead	**RAG** – Red/Amber/Green

How it works

Education is rife with acronyms, abbreviations and buzz words. It can be difficult for a teacher to keep up, let alone our students! Acronyms can support feedback, as they can enable the teacher to provide feedback quickly and efficiently. However, it is important that students fully understand what each acronym represents and understand what it means for them in terms of their progress and next steps. The table above includes the most used acronyms and abbreviations linked to feedback, but it is not exhaustive. Consistency really is key when it comes to terminology and acronyms used in the classroom and across a school. When terms are employed across a whole school, this can support learners as they are more likely to become familiar with these acronyms and abbreviations.

Top tips

- If a teacher uses WWW/EBI or the STAR method, it is a good idea to encourage students to use the same for peer assessment.
- The best abbreviations and acronyms are ones that are memorable and used regularly in the classroom.

67. Five Rs of Feedback as Actions – Tom Sherrington

| Redraft or Redo | Rehearse or Repeat | Revisit and Respond | Relearn and Retest | Research and Record |

How it works

Tom Sherrington writes:

> 'If teachers are going to have a significant impact with the feedback they give, it needs to lead to improved outcomes for students. I am increasingly convinced that feedback needs to be constituted less in terms of a review of what has gone before and more in terms of very specific actions that students should take in order to move forward. I think there are broadly five main types of actions that students should be asked to take after their work has been evaluated.'

The five types of actionable feedback are shown in the graphic above with 1. **Redraft or Redo**, 2. **Rehearse or Repeat**, 3. **Revisit and Respond**, 4. **Relearn and Retest** and 5. **Research and Record**. This approach aligns with the need for all feedback to be understandable, helpful and actionable. The examples listed by Sherrington can be combined with a range of feedback techniques in this book. You can read the complete blog post by Tom Sherrington at https://teacherhead.com/2017/12/18/fiveways-of-giving-effective-feedback-as-actions/.

Top tips

- Students should become accustomed to regularly doing something with the feedback they receive. Acting on feedback should become a consistent and productive learning habit.

- The graphic above can be put on display, visible in class books and/or a VLE (virtual learning environment), or formatted as a bookmark in order to regularly remind students of the different ways in which they can respond to feedback.

68. Feedback Finder

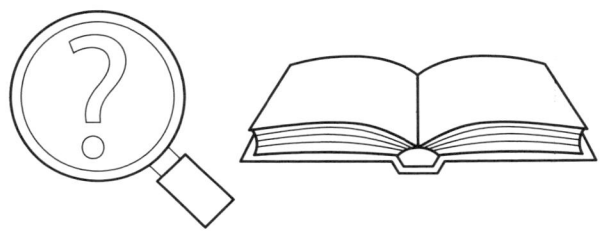

How it works

This task encourages students to find feedback and reflect on that feedback. This feedback could be from the teacher, peers, family members or using technology such as AI. Although younger students can receive feedback from multiple sources, this task is more appropriate for older students. Students need to be able to carefully reflect on the feedback and consider if it is accurate, helpful and actionable. This also helps to build a positive mindset and attitude towards feedback – that it should be sought after and embraced, in contrast to feedback being dreaded or ignored. Students should be seeking feedback and demonstrating a desire to improve, progress and learn.

Top tips

- It is important that the feedback students have sought is understandable, helpful and actionable (and it must be relevant and accurate).

- Parents can be equipped with resources, such as 'Knowledge Organisers' and/or 'Success Criteria' or mark schemes to help them ensure that the feedback they are giving to their child is reliable and helpful (some parents can lack confidence in giving feedback to their children, hence the need for support materials and resources).

- In addition to finding feedback, students should be encouraged to seek help if they need it and not be reluctant to do so.

69. Feedback Deadlines and Dates

How it works

'Feedback Deadlines and Dates' are designed to ensure leaders, teachers, students and parents all know when feedback will be given and received. This approach to feedback takes place after assessments, mock or trial exams, and tests. Across a teaching staff, the marking amount varies significantly. Some teachers will have more classes (or larger class sizes) than others, whereas some subjects (because of the nature of the content) will take longer to assess (for example, English and humanities). Setting a deadline that gives all teachers enough time to assess or moderate work enables everyone to work towards the same date. Leaders at all levels should not be allowed to request teachers to finish their assessment marking before this deadline, but teachers must ensure the deadline is met. No results are to be given to any classes or individuals before the agreed whole-staff date (this will naturally be after the deadline date for assessing). Students and parents are to be clearly instructed not to request information about exams, test scores, grades or answers prior to the deadline date. This removes pressure from teachers to provide results as soon as possible and instead to work within a manageable timeframe allowing enough time for their careful consideration and moderation.

At my previous school, there were several dates placed on the school calendar in advance. The dates included the exam schedule followed by a deadline date for when exams had to be assessed by (ensuring sufficient time for all staff members) and a date on which results could be provided.

I found this set of dates to be extremely helpful. As head of department, I did not ask my team for any data or results before the deadline date and no one requested that information from me. Everyone respected and followed the guidelines.

> **Top tips**
>
> - It is essential that deadline dates are communicated clearly (and with plenty of notice) to leaders, teachers, students and parents.

70. 'Tick Trick' – Adam Boxer

Es i i'r siopau penwythnos duwethaf efo fy teulu.

How it works

A simple but powerful feedback technique created by science teacher, author and co-founder of Carousel Learning, Adam Boxer. The 'Tick Trick' can be used with answers on mini-whiteboards or paper-based quizzing. Instead of the teacher simply providing the correct answers for students to put a tick or cross against, a series of ticks are up for grabs as the teacher goes through the process, structure or working out. The 'Tick Trick' can help the teacher and student to identify exactly where they went wrong in the process. The example shown was a sentence that students were asked to write in Welsh (second language). The student has used the past tense correctly and included accurate vocabulary, but there is a spelling error, and the final word requires a letter change. This encourages students to meaningfully and carefully engage with the feedback provided. It also enables the teacher to gain a more insightful check for understanding. Boxer has stated, 'As with most of the other strategies I like to recommend, it also doesn't require much extra work, you don't need to plan it out or prepare any resources or whatever, it's just a slight shift to the way you deliver feedback in the moment' (Boxer, 2023). There is a link at the end of this book to direct you to the original blog post by Boxer entitled 'Feedback: hitting home'.

Top tips
- This can be used for peer assessment, although arguably self-assessment is preferable as it allows learners to see for themselves exactly where they have gone wrong (if they have).

- There are some subjects this lends itself to very well; for example, to maths, science, MFL and English. Maths teacher and podcast host Craig Barton is a fan of this technique. Barton writes, 'The Tick Trick forces students to focus on their working out and not just the final answer' (Barton, 2024).

71. ChatGPT (AI)

> Create a quiz on Theme 1 Marketing and People for Edexcel A-level Business students.

> Here's a quiz on **Theme 1: Marketing and People** tailored for **Edexcel A-level Business** students. It includes a mix of multiple-choice, short answer, and application questions to test understanding of key concepts.

How it works

The debate rages on whether AI will help or hinder education. ChatGPT (and other AI platforms such as Microsoft Copilot or Gemini by Google) can assist teachers and students with the creation of teaching, learning and revision materials, in addition to supporting teacher workload. When instructed, ChatGPT can create a quiz based on a specific topic or unit targeted at a key stage or year group (it can also be instructed to focus on a specific exam board). It can create multiple-choice, short answer, application or examination-style questions. The speed with which ChatGPT can create a quiz is very impressive, and the questions can also be altered if required. As well as creating a set of quiz questions, an answer sheet can be provided (there are options to download these as a Word document or PDF, or they can be embedded within an online quiz). The quiz questions and answer sheets can be used within a lesson to check for understanding, rehearse information or as an opportunity for retrieval practice. Students can peer or self-assess their answers using the ChatGPT-generated answer sheets.

> **Top tips**
>
> - It is important to remember that AI can and does make errors, so monitoring and checking for accuracy is essential. The more detail provided, the better the accuracy and quality.
> - The teacher could model and demonstrate to the class how a quiz can be created, with answers provided, so that learners know how to use AI to help them with their studies effectively with retrieval practice, in contrast to using AI for copying and transferring information.

72. Traffic Light Collection Piles

How it works

This is a feedback and self-assessment technique from my classroom. When students submit their class books or essays at the end of a lesson, they can place them in a pile to represent how they feel about their work using the red, amber, green (RAG) rating. If their work is placed in the red pile (this can be identified with a red tray or piece of red card), this shows the student struggled with the work or would like further support. The amber pile is for students who do not require specific teacher input or support but are lacking in confidence or have some doubts and/or further questions. The green pile is for students feeling happy and confident with the work they are submitting. The RAG rating system does not always accurately reflect students' level of understanding or ability. A student may have written a model answer but perhaps put their work in the amber pile because they lack confidence, or a student could place their book in the green pile, unaware of errors they have made. My students were not always required to submit work in this way, but when they did, I would immediately visit the red pile of books to find out who needed my help and identify how I could support them. I would also review books in the amber and green piles, but it was insightful for me to gauge students' level of self-awareness and confidence.

Top tips

- It is important to clearly explain to students what each pile represents and provide students with enough time to think about where to place their work.
- This can be useful for whole-class feedback; for example, 'Several books in the red pile were unsure about this question, so I will go over this now.'
- Collection trays/piles could also be organised into two categories. For example, 'Got it' and 'Help needed'.

73. Feedback First, Grade Later

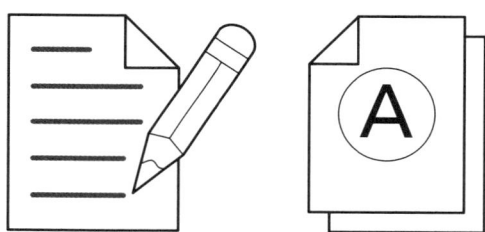

How it works

Students can tend to focus on scores, percentages and grades when they receive a marked assessment rather than the feedback provided. Grades can be useful data for students to have, but prioritising grades over feedback is not helpful. 'Comment-only' marking is an approach to feedback where learners are given feedback, and the grades are withheld or given later. Students can find this frustrating, but it is important that they understand the need to meaningfully engage with and reflect upon feedback. The EEF Feedback Guidance Report (2021) stated:

> 'On grading, there is evidence which suggests that grades alone may not improve pupil performance and that they are better replaced by comments. However, more recent studies have demonstrated mixed results following the provision of comments instead of grades. Perhaps giving a grade alone could still provide information to progress learning providing preparatory work has been done to ensure that the learner already knows what that grade means and what improvements they need to make on specific types of task—and in that subject generally—to reach the next grade. Careful planning may also be needed to ensure that pupils are not disheartened or distracted by the grade.'

When the task is formative, the feedback is essential, as it should continue to move learning forwards. When a task is summative (for example, a final exam), then a grade is more appropriate. A final grade is secured based on all questions completed and dependent on mark schemes and grade boundaries. Therefore, awarding grades for individual questions is not always an accurate description of these grades.

> **Top tips**
>
> - The teacher should use their professional judgement (individually or as a department) to decide when comment-only marking is appropriate and when to assign grades.

74. Match the Marking

the cat is big.	Spelling mistake.
I went to the park	Capital letter needed at the start of the sentence.
The bus is redd.	Full stop needed at the end of the sentence.

How it works

This task was designed for students to match the feedback to the correct example, as shown above. This allows students to identify the mistakes and become familiar with feedback comments or criteria. The example above was used with primary learners, but this task could be adapted for older learners, with more complex examples and feedback linked to assessment objectives and mark schemes. The feedback could match up to the relevant mistake or precise praise could be matched to the relevant example. There are lots of variations of 'Match the Marking'; for example, students could be shown an error and then go on to select the relevant literacy or marking codes. This can be completed as an individual task, in pairs or groups, or as a whole-class discussion with mistakes shown on the board or using a visualiser. To make the task more challenging, the marking comments could be removed for students so they can find, mark and fix the mistakes themselves.

Top tips

- The examples provided should be linked to the learning intention and can also be an opportunity to demonstrate common misconceptions or keywords that can be difficult to spell.
- This could be a sorting task with matching cards or adapted as a digital task.

75. Austin's Butterfly – Ron Berger

How it works

Throughout this book I have referenced Ron Berger as his work has hugely influenced and inspired my classroom practice. Berger features in a video clip, fondly known as 'Austin's Butterfly' (available to view via YouTube). In the short video, Berger shares the work – a sketch of a butterfly – by a first-grade elementary student (Austin from Boise, Idaho, United States) with a group of young students. Berger shows the students how Austin was able to improve and transform his original sketch by acting on the kind, specific and helpful critique he received from his peers (not the teacher). Without revealing any spoilers, it is safe to say the transformation and progression demonstrated by Austin is very impressive! This video has been shared widely with teachers, but I believe students should watch it too, to help them appreciate the power of peer critique. If students doubt the power and impact of peer critique and feedback, then this video can challenge that perception.

> **Top tips**
> - The video can be shared to classes or shown during an assembly. This should be followed by time provided for students to reflect and discuss the video clip.

- There are lots of powerful messages that can be taken from this short video clip; as well as recognising the value and effectiveness of peer assessment, it can encourage students not to settle but to keep going.

76. Guess the Feedback

First draft	Second draft
Daisy went for a walk along the beach, it was her favourite place to go because she loved the sea, sand and she had lots of happy memories at the beach.	*It was a cool but bright morning when Daisy went for a stroll along the beach. She loved the sounds of the sea from the crashing waves to whistling wind.*
What feedback do you think was provided after the first draft to create the second draft? Extension task: What further feedback would you add to improve the second draft?	

How it works

This is a task that enables students to see how feedback can improve a piece of work and a learner (as can be achieved through viewing the 'Austin's Butterfly' video; see the previous technique). Students are provided with an example of classwork (this can be projected onto the board or printed) and a similar example is placed next to it that has been significantly improved as a result of feedback. The task requires the students to review both examples and decide what feedback was provided to improve the first example. Students could complete this individually, in pairs or in small groups. This can help learners to see the impact of acting on feedback, as the changes and progress are made visible and the feedback is discussed.

Top tips

- This task could be combined with 'Think-Pair-Share', where learners reflect on the original piece of work to discuss and decide on what feedback has been provided and what further feedback could be given.
- The example above is based on a primary task, but it could be adapted for older students with a focus on exam answers in order to demonstrate the difference between marks and levels awarded.

77. Confidence Rating Scale

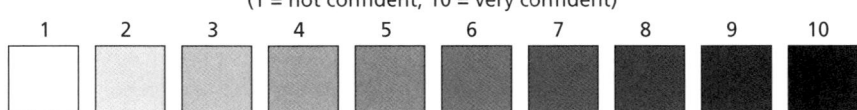

How it works

Students can rate their levels of confidence before, during and/or after a task, unit and/or assessment to self-reflect. The confidence ratings could be numbered as shown with the example above. Colours such as red, amber and green could be used to represent different levels of confidence linked to the RAG ratings. The scale could include terms such as very/not very confident. An alternative to this (which could be more suitable for younger learners or some learners with SEND) could be the use of emojis/smiley faces. Similar to the 'Emoji Exit Ticket' (technique 61), an important element of the reflection is being able to explain or justify what number, image or word they have selected to rate their confidence. MFL expert, author and CEO of the language gym Gianfranco Conti has written about confidence ratings. Conti writes:

> 'In modern language classrooms, we work hard to help our students master vocabulary and grammar, but how often do we ask them *how confident* they are in their knowledge? Confidence rating scales are a simple but powerful way to do just that. By getting students to reflect on how certain they are when recalling a word or grammar rule, we give them the chance to take ownership of their learning. ... Confidence rating scales are easy to use, cost nothing, and take very little time. Yet they can dramatically improve how our students learn and revise. They also give us teachers valuable insight: not just what students got right, but what they're unsure about—even if they're not saying it out loud.'

Top tips

- Students should compare their confidence ratings with the overall results, as they may have lacked confidence or overestimated their ability, knowledge and/or skills.
- Online quizzing platforms such as Google Forms enable users to easily create a digital confidence scale for users to select.

78. 'Go-To Glossary'

Planets
Mercury
Venus
Earth
Mars
Jupiter
Saturn
Uranus
Neptune

Earth and Space

Vocabulary

Astronaut – A person who is trained to travel in a spacecraft.

Atmosphere – The gases held by gravity around Earth and around other planets.

Planet – Large natural objects that orbit or travel around stars.

Constellation – A group of stars in the sky.

Galaxy – A collection of thousands to billions of stars held together by gravity.

Orbit – The curved path that a planet, satellite or spacecraft moves along as it circles around another object.

How it works

A 'Go-To Glossary' or word mat can be used to support students when they are required to spell complex or difficult words (tier-three vocabulary) correctly. The resource can be used as a form of pre-emptive feedback, as students should regularly be encouraged to double check spellings of keywords during tasks, before they submit their classwork. A 'Go-To Glossary' should be a document that isn't just stuck in books but instead is something students regularly 'go to' for checking and correcting. The glossary can contain all the keywords from the unit, as shown in the primary science example above.

> **Top tips**
>
> - There are other ways the 'Go-To Glossary' can be used in a lesson; for example, during paired quizzing. Students quiz their partner on spellings and/or definitions of key terms. The glossary allows students to provide each other with immediate feedback.
> - The 'Go-To Glossary' can be used at home with parents to support spellings or for retrieval practice quizzing.

79. Redrafting

How it works

Redrafting was identified as one of the Five Actionable Rs by Tom Sherrington (technique 67), but it is worthy of further discussion. It is important that redrafting is an efficient and effective use of student time. Redrafting is an actionable task for students to improve a piece of classwork based on feedback from the teacher or peer, but the advice from Dylan Wiliam (2017) – that feedback should improve the learner not the work – is key when redrafting work. There can be different areas to focus on when redrafting, from improving literacy errors and including a wider range of vocabulary, to adding more depth, detail, explanation or examples. The purpose of redrafting could be to make the piece of work more interesting for the reader or to alter the structure. Overall, the main aim is to improve accuracy and quality. It can potentially be very time-consuming and frustrating for the learner to redraft a whole essay, answer or story, so focusing on specific sections or paragraphs can be more manageable and help to improve the students' skill sets, not just their work. This links back to the 'Yellow Box Method' (technique 23).

Top tips

- Students can begin with redrafting and improving sentences and gradually build up to paragraphs and extended sections of work.

Feedback: Resource Guide

> - Students can use AI to help redraft and improve their work, but it is essential they only seek feedback from AI in contrast to getting AI to do all the hard work for them. If students are using AI, it is important they are transparent through clearly explaining or demonstrating how they have used it.

80. Spelling Logs

How it works

There are different techniques throughout this book that can be used to provide feedback and support students with literacy and, specifically, spellings. One method is for students to record spelling errors, in a log, a journal, the back of a class book or digitally. The purpose of this is to provide students with an opportunity to practise spellings, and the spelling log should be used to avoid repeating the same spelling errors. The spelling logs could also be used for pair or self-quizzing. Students are quizzed on words they have previously spelled incorrectly. Once the spelling has been successfully mastered, this can also be recorded in the spelling log.

Spelling Shed is a leading evidence-based platform supporting the teaching of spelling and contains a wide range of resources, strategies and approaches to teach and assess spellings. The Spelling Shed guidance (n.d.) has stated the following:

> 'One of the changes from the 2017 scheme is the removal of the Look - Say - Cover - Write - Check sheets. Our research has led us to remove them as they are often used as a time filler or for handwriting practice but have little impact on spelling. Research has shown that as little as 20 minutes per week of word study including discussing spelling patterns, morphological exploration and orthographic mapping can have a bigger impact on spelling than the repetitive daily copying of word lists.'

I agree with this as the 'Look – Say – Cover – Write – Check' approach to spellings enables learners to hold on to the spelling of a key word temporarily in their working memory but does not guarantee at a later date that the student will be able to correctly retrieve the spelling of that word.

> **Top tips**
>
> - For more information about the science of spelling, visit www.spellingshed.com/en-gb/.
> - The spelling log should be a living document that students review and refer to regularly, in contrast to recording something without meaningfully engaging with it.

81. Watch and Wait

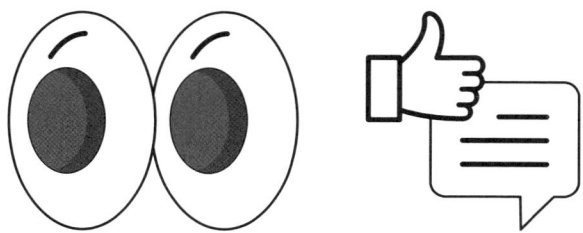

How it works

Providing sufficient 'wait time' after a question has been asked has long been an area of my classroom development, and by observing other teachers, I have noticed a 'teacher's 30 seconds' can be closer to five seconds than 30 (although not always!). The 'Watch and Wait' approach to feedback is inspired by the work of my former colleague and friend Louise Vann, as cited in her EYFS case study in *Feedback: Strategies to Support Teacher Workload and Improve Pupil Progress* (Jones, 2024). Louise Vann writes:

> 'Many times, I have bulldozed into some child-led learning with my preconceived teacher feedback questions, only to be given the cold shoulder or having disrupted the flow of learning which has then been abandoned by the child. I have learnt that careful questioning and timely interactions are the name of the game. Often watching and waiting for a child to speak to you means they have given you the golden ticket to enter their play. It is then up to the practitioner to quickly think about where that child is, what that child needs and what opportunities are there to move learning forwards. This is all skilfully done on the spot and in the moment.'

Students need time to solve problems, and by providing think and wait time prior to giving feedback, this can help to foster independence and resilience. On reflection, I can recall opportunities in a lesson where I have prematurely provided feedback or instructions to my students, always well intentioned, but perhaps at the cost of them thinking hard, solving a problem or self-checking and correcting.

Top tips

- It can be difficult for the teacher to 'Watch and Wait', as teachers we have a natural instinct to help and support our students. During the waiting time, it can be helpful to record any notes or points to later refer to when providing the feedback to learners.

82. Colour Coded Feedback

Colour	Feedback
Blue	Work has gone far above and beyond and is exceptional.
Green	All learning tasks have been completed to the required standard. Academy presentation standards have been met.
Yellow	Has not met one of the green expectations.
Red/pink	Learning tasks have not been completed to the required standard or academy presentation standards are consistently not met.
Orange	There is a misconception. Self-check and, if unsure, check with teacher.

How it works

Colour coding feedback can be helpful for the teacher and student to identify exactly what the feedback is targeting (for example, one colour for content, another for literacy, a specific colour to highlight strengths and another to highlight areas for development). Colour coding feedback can also be used to show who is providing the feedback. For example, the use of a purple pen for self-assessment, green for peer assessment and blue for teacher assessment. The example above is from The Cheadle Academy and supports their teaching, learning and feedback policies. Teachers can use the colour coding feedback live in a lesson or post lesson when reviewing student work. Obviously, the colour of the pen is not as important as the quality of the feedback, or what the learner does with the feedback, but it can serve a useful purpose. It is advisable for a colour-coded approach to be consistent across a school to avoid any confusion for learners. The same colours could also be applied when reviewing work digitally, via Google Classroom, for example, ensuring the feedback from the peer and teacher is visible.

Feedback: Resource Guide

> **Top tips**
> - If specific colour pens are being used for teacher, peer and self-assessment, then be sure to stock up on the colour pens!
> - Students must have access to the colour code chart. It could be on display in classrooms so it is always visible.

83. Comments Banks

> **A-level psychology comments banks – AO1 knowledge and understanding**
> Needs to include more detail on case studies (e.g. HM, KF) to support model explanations.
> Confused the features of MSM and WMM – review the capacity, duration and coding of stores.
> Key terminology (e.g. central executive, phonological loop) needs clearer definition.

How it works

I have used 'Comments Banks' when I have been tasked to write hundreds of extensive written reports for students and their parents. 'Comments Banks' contain a collection of statements related to learning, behaviour, motivation and progress, etc. Using this technique is workload efficient, but the task still requires a lot of careful attention from the teacher. For each individual student I would select the relevant statements (in addition to some personalised comments), and this would form the report. It was a smart and efficient approach to a lengthy and demanding task. 'Comments Banks' can be applied to feedback, especially when the teacher will be referring to specific success criteria and a mark scheme (the likelihood of repeating feedback comments among a class is high, too). The teacher will think carefully about the statement in terms of its phrasing and language, the links to the learning intentions and assessment criteria, and how the statements from the 'Comments Banks' can provide understandable, helpful and actionable feedback to learners. They can also be used to support peer assessment, where students select the relevant statements to give to their partner.

Top tips

- It is advisable to create or discuss 'Comments Banks' as a department or team, with scope to allow for adaptation for the classroom context (the example above was generated by ChatGPT).
- Students (and parents) should understand that 'Comments Banks' aren't just copied and pasted to save time but instead provide meaningful, personalised and relevant feedback to support progress.

84. Feedback Tracker

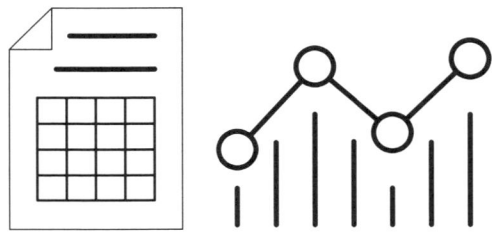

How it works

Tracking, recording and analysing data is something that teachers and leaders within schools do to monitor progress and identify any trends or patterns. Older students can be tasked to record and track their feedback and scores and then reflect on that data to assess their improvements and identify areas they need to focus on. For exam classes, this can be a record of scores to specific exam questions or units. Students can then see for themselves if they are struggling to gain full marks on the eight-mark question, for example, or if they perform better on quizzes for a specific unit. This can be as simple as regularly filling in a page, the back of a book or a digital spreadsheet. The 'Feedback Tracker' could be shared with the teacher to help them adapt their lessons accordingly, based on what students know and don't know. The tracker could just be a record for the students to give them ownership of and responsibility for their learning, as well as guiding their independent study and revision. This can be a time-efficient method for students to be able to regularly review their results and progress.

Top tips

- The 'Feedback Tracker' can be part of a 'Feedback Journal' (see technique 59) and can be used in combination with 'Exam Wrappers' (see technique 37) and 'Flashback Feedback' (see technique 17).
- There are many online tools and websites that students can use to record, track and revisit their feedback data.

85. Chunk, Check, Correct

How it works

Chunking, also known in cognitive science as the Segmenting Principle, suggests that learners can benefit when material is presented to them in segments (or smaller, related chunks) rather than as a continuous block. Chunking is often applied in the classroom to support the limitations of working memory capacity, with explanations or instructions broken down into manageable chunks. I have embraced the chunking concept with feedback to support my classes with peer and self-assessment. Through peer or self-checking and correcting, students can identify errors or misconceptions before the work is submitted to the teacher. However, it can be easy for learners to overlook or miss errors and misconceptions. Through 'chunking the checking', students can be instructed to focus on a specific area. For example, the class can be instructed to review their work with a focus on literacy, or within that, a specific focus on spellings. Alternatively, this approach could be more content or criteria based. This has prioritised focused feedback, so learners are able to check and correct and then move on to the next chunk/area. As students develop and gain experience with peer and self-assessment, I tend to move away from this approach, but I have found it helpful with younger students (specifically at key stage three) and with tasks that involve extended answers or essays.

Top tips

- This can be linked with 'Peer Assessment with Immediate Impact' (technique 26).

Final Thoughts

I began my teaching career in 2009. I have many memories of taking boxes of class books home in my car to mark over the weekend. I recall piles of exam papers and essays on my desk, and feeling completely overwhelmed. I also felt resentful of the time spent in the evenings and weekends writing comments in books that should have been spent much more healthily, with my friends, family or just on hobbies. Despite my frustrations, I accepted that this was simply a part of the job. Teaching is incredibly rewarding and enjoyable. It is a privilege to be a teacher, and I told myself that no job is perfect. While no job is indeed perfect, there was no justification for spending unnecessary time, effort and energy on a practice that was not guaranteed to help my students and was having a negative impact on my wellbeing.

Teacher wellbeing needs to be viewed through the lens of teacher workload. Workload and wellbeing are inextricably linked in this profession. Feedback has been an undeniable contributing factor to teacher burnout and excessive workload. Those days need to be firmly put behind us. Teachers are required to spend time planning and preparing lessons, as well as undertaking pastoral responsibilities, carrying out administrative duties and, of course, actually teaching! If feedback absorbs too much time, then other aspects of teaching will suffer. None of this is to dismiss the role of feedback (far from it!), but instead we should view feedback as one piece of a teaching and learning jigsaw puzzle. Feedback is an important piece of that puzzle, but only one piece. There are others to consider.

Throughout my teaching career I have observed a shift in focus and attitude towards feedback. At a previous school, the senior leaders had a sensible approach to feedback, always considering the implications of policies on teachers, students and parents. During this time I became fascinated by the literature and evidence base on feedback. I was in a position, as head of department, to contribute to the whole-school approach to feedback and create the departmental policy. This experience was positive and enlightening. It has influenced my decision to focus on feedback in my writing, presentations and consultancy roles. I feel a strong sense of optimism about the profession (although it continues to face challenges) because we are living in an evidence-rich age. Research has never been more accessible and widely discussed among educators. This is evident from the widespread access to research and the emergence of research-focused events, books, blogs and articles published concentrating on evidence-based practices.

There is a vast amount of feedback techniques and resources in this book. Some will be more relevant and suitable for your classroom context than others. It is for you, the teacher, to reflect on, select and trial a feedback technique in your classroom. I believe teachers should embrace a variety of feedback options and techniques in addition to embracing the many benefits of new technologies in the field. In the foreword of the EEF Feedback Guidance Report (2021) Dylan Wiliam argued the following: 'The existing research does not tell teachers how to guarantee the feedback they give their students will be effective, and probably never will; teaching is just far too complex for this ever to be likely.' This is a point worth remembering, as evidence doesn't provide a paint-by-numbers guide to feedback, and surely as professionals this is not something to be desired. Instead, evidence can provide useful insight, guidance and 'best bets'. Evidence can and should always be combined with teacher experience and expertise!

Across the UK and internationally, there is a recognition of the excessive workload and unrealistic demands that have been placed upon teachers. There can now be seen a clear change in direction towards using evidence-informed teaching and learning methods that support teacher workload and help move learning forwards. The examples throughout this book are what I like to refer to as 'evidence-inspired', and always take into consideration teacher workload and student progression. Providing feedback should be an efficient process for the teacher, and so the techniques and approaches used should be workload friendly, sustainable and insightful. Feedback should be effective for the learner, and this is possible when the feedback communicated is understandable, helpful and actionable, and where the student is willing to engage and revise their work in order to develop their skills and knowledge.

It has been a privilege to observe a wide range of lessons across primary, secondary and further education. I have been able to learn a lot from all teachers. I believe as a profession we should aim to learn from and support one another. We can do so with the focus on feedback.

Thank you for taking the time to read my book, and I sincerely hope it has a positive impact on your classroom practice.

Kate

Bibliography

Ali, A. (n.d.) *Editing tabs.* Available at: www.trythisteaching.com/2016/12/editing-tabs/

Barton, C. (2024) *#56 Try these four different ways of going through the answers.* Available at: https://tipsforteachers.substack.com/p/56-try-these-four-different-ways

Berger, R. (2003) *An Ethic of Excellence: Building a Culture of Craftsmanship with Students.* Heinemann Educational Books.

Boxer, A. (2023) *Feedback: hitting home.* Available at: https://achemicalorthodoxy.co.uk/2023/03/30/feedback-hitting-home/

Class Teaching. (2015) *Gallery critique.* Available at: https://classteaching.wordpress.com/2015/06/04/gallery-critique/

Conti, G. (2025) *Using confidence rating scales to deepen vocabulary and grammar learning in the MFL classroom.* Available at: https://gianfrancoconti.com/2025/04/24/using-confidence-rating-scales-to-deepen-vocabulary-and-grammar-learning-in-the-mfl-classroom/

Department for Education. (2013) *Data protection in schools.* Available at: www.gov.uk/guidance/data-protection-in-schools

Education Endowment Foundation (EEF). (April, 2018 and updated October, 2021). *Metacognition and self-regulated learning.* Available at: https://educationendowmentfoundation.org.uk/education-evidence/guidance-reports/metacognition

Education Endowment Foundation (EEF). (2021) *Teacher Feedback to Improve Pupil Learning.* Guidance Report.

Hattie, J., and Timperley, H. (2007) 'The power of feedback.' *Review of Educational Research,* 77(1), 81–112.

Jones, K. (2018) Love to Teach: Research and Resources for Every Classroom. John Catt Educational.

Jones, K. (2024) *Feedback: Strategies to Support Teacher Workload and Improve Pupil Progress.* John Catt Educational.

Lovett, M. C. (2013) 'Make exams worth more than the grade.' In: Kaplan, M., Silver, N., LaVaque-Manty, D., and Meizlish, D. *Using Reflection and Metacognition to Improve Student Learning: Across the Disciplines, Across the Academy*. Stylus.

Kirby, J. (2015) *Knowledge organisers*. Available at: https://joe-kirby.com/2015/03/28/knowledge-organisers/

Leitner Flashcards. (n.d.) *Leitner flashcards*. Available at: https://leitnerflashcards.com/

Lemov, D. (2021) *Teach Like a Champion 3.0: 63 Techniques that Put Students on the Path to College*. Jossey-Bass.

Lyman, F. (1981) 'The responsive classroom discussions: the inclusion of all students.' A. Anderson (ed.), *Mainstreaming Digest*, College Park: University of Maryland Press, pp. 109–113.

Oracy Education Commission. (2024) *We need to talk*. Available at: https://oracyeducationcommission.co.uk/wp-content/uploads/2024/10/We-need-to-talk-2024.pdf

researchED. (2018) *Comparative judgement: the next big revolution in assessment?* Available at: https://researched.org.uk/2018/07/06/comparative-judgement-the-next-big-revolution-in-assessment-2/

Sinek, S. (2021) *Start with Why: How Great Leaders Inspire Everyone to Take Action*. Penguin.

Spelling Shed. (n.d.) *Spelling Shed guidance*. Available at: www.spellingshed.com/en-us/scheme-guidanceTeacher Teachers Talk Radio. (n.d.) Available at: www.ttradio.org/

Thornton, G. (2016) *Marking crib sheet and whole class feedback*. Available at: https://mrthorntonteach.com/2016/04/08/marking-crib-sheet/

Tom Sherrington. (2017) *#FiveWays of giving effective feedback as actions*. Available at: https://teacherhead.com/2017/12/18/fiveways-of-giving-effective-feedback-as-actions/

Toolkit. (n.d.) *Yellow box methodology*. Available at: www.teachertoolkit.co.uk/2018/05/19/yellow-box-methodology/

Wiliam, D., and Leahy, S. (2015) *Embedding Formative Assessment: Practical Techniques for K-12 Classrooms*. Learning Sciences International.

Wiliam, D. (2017) 'Assessment, marking and feedback.' In: Hendrick, C., and Macpherson, R. *What Does This Look Like in the Classroom?: Bridging the Gap Between Research and Practice*. John Catt Educational, pp. 22–44.